Also by Donald E. Worcester

The Three Worlds of Latin America
MEXICO, CENTRAL AMERICA AND SOUTH AMERICA

MAKERS OF LATIN AMERICA

Makers of

LATIN AMERICA

by *Donald E. Worcester*

CHAIRMAN, DEPARTMENT OF HISTORY
TEXAS CHRISTIAN UNIVERSITY

New York: E. P. DUTTON & CO., INC.

Map drawings by J. E. Massey

To Concho

CONTENTS

MAKERS OF LATIN AMERICA

INTRODUCTION

The discovery and conquest of the New World, beginning in 1492 with Columbus's first voyage, were among the most dramatic and important events in modern history. The Western Hemisphere was peopled by Indian tribes of varying degrees of cultural development, from the most primitive hunters and gatherers to the complex societies of the Incas, Aztecs, and Mayas. All were Stone Age peoples, for metals were little used except in ornamentation by the highest civilizations. Though the Indians were numerous and courageous, they were conquered by a relatively few Europeans. Tribal hatreds were so strong that the Indians gladly aided the Europeans in the destruction of their traditional foes, as when the Tlascalans helped Cortez in conquering the Aztecs. The Europeans also had the advantages of firearms, steel weapons, horses, and military discipline, all of which the natives lacked.

The Spaniards quickly found the most valuable regions—those with the high native civilizations—and occupied them. They built great cities, and established schools and universities. Administering these far-off lands and strange peoples posed many problems for the kings and their councilors.

What to do with the Indians was a basic problem with moral as well as economic overtones. Though Spanish monarchs worried for a century over their right to occupy New World lands, conquest and settlement were not delayed by their doubts. Some Spaniards and Portuguese favored outright enslavement of the Indians, while others, such as Father Bartolomé de las Casas, protested that the Indians were rational beings and had souls and that slavery was therefore morally wrong. The early Spanish solution to the problem was the *encomienda* system, under which Indians were "commended" to the care of Spaniards who were to Christianize and civilize them, and to pay their "tribute" or head tax in exchange for their labor. Presumably the Indians would

13

eventually become Spanish citizens. The system was theoretically humane, but it became the means of forcing the Indians to work against their will. Efforts to abolish the *encomienda* were fiercely resisted by the conquerors and their descendants in the sixteenth century, though by the eighteenth century it had gradually disappeared. The Portuguese did not develop a similar system in Brazil, but the efforts of the Jesuits to end Indian slavery there were violently resisted by the planters. The Indians of Brazil were primitive and weak, and even as slaves they made an unsuitable labor force. The Portuguese imported large numbers of slaves from their African colonies, and Negro slaves were largely responsible for Brazil's economic development.

In both Spanish and Portuguese America a class and caste system developed in the sixteenth century. At the apex of society, government, and the Church were the Peninsulares and Reinhões, Spaniards and Portuguese born in Europe. Below them were the Creoles, people supposedly of pure European descent who had been born in the New World. The mestizos, or mixed bloods, were far below these two classes, but were next in the social scale. After them came the Indians, and at the lowest rung of the social ladder were the Negro slaves.

Late in 1807 Napoleon sent troops into Portugal, and the royal family fled to Brazil. In 1815 Brazil was raised to the rank of kingdom, co-equal with Portugal. Six years later, Dom João VI returned to Portugal, leaving his son, Dom Pedro, as regent. The Portuguese government tried to force Brazil to become a mere colony again, but in 1822 Dom Pedro became emperor of an independent Brazil. Compared to most of the Spanish colonies, Brazil's independence movement was easy, largely because of the skillful leadership of José Bonifácio de Andrada. There was little bloodshed or destruction, and there was no legacy of militarism, as happened in Mexico and elsewhere.

After his troops took Portugal, Napoleon forced Ferdinand VII of Spain to abdicate, and placed his own brother Joseph on the Spanish throne. The Spanish people formed juntas of self-government and fought to preserve Spain for Ferdinand, but in

1810 French troops completed the conquest of the whole country. Throughout Spanish America men who yearned for independence seized the opportunity, and created juntas of self-government of their own. To deceive those persons who were still loyal to the absent king, they claimed that they were fighting to preserve their lands for Ferdinand VII.

By 1812 the Spanish guerrillas had recovered most of the country from the French, although Ferdinand was still a prisoner of Napoleon. The Cortes, or Parliament, that drew up a liberal constitution in 1812 included Creole representatives from Spanish America. The constitution and the opportunity to be represented in the Spanish government raised the hopes of many Spanish Americans for peaceful relations within the Empire, but these hopes were vain. In 1814 Ferdinand recovered his throne. Ferdinand was an absolutist, and the idea of a constitutional monarchy was completely unacceptable to him. His harsh treatment of his colonies and of Spanish liberals who had saved his crown for him strengthened the desire for independence. In 1820 Spanish troops preparing to embark for the colonial wars mutinied and forced Ferdinand to restore the constitution. This mutiny ended Spanish attempts to reconquer the colonies.

After independence the Spanish American nations had great difficulty in achieving political stability and economic development. In the colonial period there had been only four major divisions, the viceroyalties of New Spain (Mexico), New Granada (Venezuela, Colombia, and Panama), Peru, and Río de la Plata. These were fragmented into eighteen states. In all of them was a small, landowning aristocracy that dominated government and society.

Because Creoles had been excluded from high office in Church and State during the colonial period, they did not develop a sense of civic responsibility. After independence their attitude did not change, and this political irresponsibility on the part of the wealthy and influential class permitted adventurers to seize the governments. In most of the new states the landowning "oligarchs" who had the power to establish stable and effective governments remained unconcerned as long as they were not molested.

After independence the Spanish Americans displayed a tremendous faith in constitutions, and expected them somehow to work miracles. Half a century of fruitless experimentation produced only cynicism. In the second half of the nineteenth century "economic development" became the panacea for all national ills. Governments competed with one another to attract foreign capital. Again the result was disillusioning, for many countries found later that aliens controlled their economies.

In the twentieth century an intense economic nationalism developed, which was characterized by such slogans as "Mexico for the Mexicans." Latin America is a place of extremely rapid population growth, and it is necessary to increase production considerably each year merely to prevent the standard of living from falling even lower. The problems of economic development are tremendous, for they include cultural as well as physical obstacles. One of the cultural obstacles is the preference for land over other types of property. Land remains the hallmark of social quality in most regions, though this attitude is slowly changing. Some countries, such as Mexico and Brazil, have made considerable progress in industrialization. Others are trying to move in the same direction, but for all of them the way is difficult and the obstacles are numerous.

It has not been possible within a limited space to include all Latin Americans whose careers are noteworthy, nor has it been possible to include representatives of every Latin American nation. Those chosen, however, have had a marked impact on their societies. The first group includes four Mexicans of the colonial and independence periods. Two, Antonio de Mendoza and Bishop Manuel Abad y Queipo, were born in Spain. Don Carlos Sigüenza y Góngora was Mexico's leading scholar of the colonial era; José María Morelos was a priest, revolutionary hero, and statesman.

The second group is of three Brazilians who were dedicated to the idea of improving the condition of the Indians. One was a Portuguese-born priest, Antônio Vieira; one was a Brazilian scien-

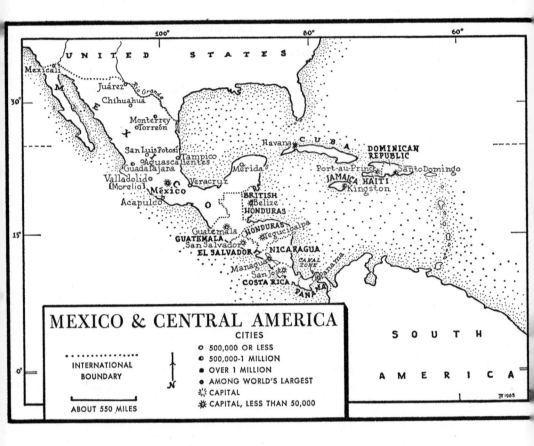

MEXICO & CENTRAL AMERICA

CITIES

- ○ 500,000 OR LESS
- ◐ 500,000-1 MILLION
- ● OVER 1 MILLION
- ◉ AMONG WORLD'S LARGEST
- ✺ CAPITAL
- ✳ CAPITAL, LESS THAN 50,000

INTERNATIONAL BOUNDARY

ABOUT 550 MILES

tist, José Bonifácio de Andrada, who spent half of his life in Portugal before returning home to become the "Architect of Brazilian Independence"; and the third, Cândido Rondon, was an army officer of Indian ancestry who spent his life working in behalf of the Indians.

José G. Artigas and Dr. José Gaspar Rodríguez de Francia were independence leaders of Uruguay and Paraguay. Artigas was the spokesman for federalism in the entire Plata region. Francia was the absolute ruler of his land. Andrés Bello and José Toribio Medina were two cultural leaders of Chile, though Bello was Venezuelan by birth. Benito Juárez and Porfirio Díaz, both largely of Indian ancestry, were presidents of Mexico in critical eras. The former was a hero of the War of the Reform (1857–1860) and the resistance to the French, and he planned economic and democratic development for Mexico. Díaz concentrated on political stability and economic development by means of foreign capital, but he scorned democracy. Bartolomé Mitre, Hipólito Irigoyen, and Evita Perón represent three different periods of Argentine history. Mitre was a military and political hero, a historian, and founder of *La Nación.* Irigoyen was the first popularly elected president of Argentina. Evita was a vital force in politics and the labor movement during the Perón era.

Antonio Guzmán Blanco, Manuel González Prada, and José Batlle y Ordóñez were political innovators in Venezuela, Peru, and Uruguay. Guzmán Blanco and Batlle were presidents of their countries, while González Prada influenced several generations of Peruvian youths through his writings.

The last two men were Brazilians, Joaquim Nabuco and Getúlio Vargas. Nabuco was one of the leading statesmen of the Empire and one of the most active abolitionists. Vargas introduced the New State and began the enormous task of transforming Brazil into a modern industrial nation.

The brief biographical sketches of these men and women indicate the wide range of achievement of Latin Americans from the Conquest to the twentieth century. They also supplement the narrative account of Latin American history presented in *The Three Worlds of Latin America* (Dutton, 1963).

D.E.W.

PART I

Viceroy, Scholar, Rebel, Priest

New Spain, modern Mexico, was the first Spanish viceroyalty in the New World. Antonio de Mendoza, as the first viceroy, was faced with the problem of establishing royal rule in the wake of the Conquest. Cortez and the other *conquistadores* had accomplished incredible feats at great sacrifice, and they expected the king to show his gratitude and confidence. Their successes had been based on daring, courage, military skill, and great ambition. Once the Conquest had been achieved, however, these very qualities made the kings more fearful of what the conquerors might do next than grateful for what they had done. Mendoza was given the unenviable task of superseding Cortez and his comrades. Mendoza's achievements were far less spectacular than those of Cortez, but they were certainly substantial.

Don Carlos Sigüenza y Góngora represents a transitional period in intellectual matters, from a period of little thought or learning to the Age of Reason. In many ways he was typical of the Baroque Age in which he lived, for his greatest ambition was to become a Jesuit priest. Though he scorned unscientific beliefs concerning the nature of comets, and some of these concepts were supported by the Jesuits, he believed in the healing powers of a deceased bishop's hat. In learning, Don Carlos adopted the "scientific approach," for he insisted on observation and proof before accepting a conclusion. In his attitude toward science he was years ahead of his contemporaries, and he was a forerunner of the Age of Reason that characterized eighteenth-century Europe.

José María Morelos was typical of many parish priests in Spanish America. Of humble births themselves, they remained with their congregations, and fought for independence from Spain. Morelos, by a combination of natural ability and determination, became the principal spokesman for Mexican liberals as well as the chief hero of the Mexican struggle for independence. Though the cause he led failed and he was executed as a traitor to Spain, the changes he sought became the program of Mexican liberals for the remainder of the nineteenth century. The idea of racial equality was especially dear to Morelos.

Whereas Mendoza represented the second wave of Europeans, who followed in the wake of the Conquest, Bishop Abad y Queipo was in the last group of Spaniards who came as officials of Church or State. He rose to the position of Bishop of Michoacán through his devotion to duty, his sense of humanity, and his natural ability. He lived during a time when the Creoles' hatred for European Spaniards reached the breaking point, and as a result he was caught in a cross fire. At a time when men were taking sides in a struggle to the death, he tried to point out to both sides the errors they were making. Both rebels and royalists were ungrateful for his efforts. Even Ferdinand VII, the monarch whose Mexican kingdom Abad tried to save for him, was cold and suspicious. Abad is an example of a devoted and loyal subject of a fickle and ungrateful king.

Antonio de Mendoza
1490–1552

At the time of Mendoza's birth in the mountain fortress of Alcalá la Real on the border of the Moslem kingdom of Granada, Spain was about to complete the Reconquest. All of Spain except Granada had been recovered from the Moslems. In 1482 Ferdinand

and Isabel began the siege of Granada. After Granada surrendered, in 1492, Spain was ready for her tremendous enterprises across the sea.

The Mendoza family was one of the most famous and powerful in all Spain, claiming descent from Roman aristocrats and even the Cid. The Mendozas were warriors, and had fought the Moslems for seven centuries. In almost any epoch there were Mendozas high in the royal service—wealthy, distinguished, and able. Antonio's father was a commander of Castilian troops in the siege of Granada.

Mendoza's youthful training was apparently in matters military, and he proved himself a capable commander. By 1526 he was serving Emperor Charles V (King Charles I of Spain) in diplomacy. In the meantime much had happened in the New World. The conquest of the Aztecs had given Charles the kingdom of New Spain, a valuable possession, although the greatest silver mines had not yet been discovered.

The task of governing far-off, unknown lands and non-Christian peoples was not a simple one, and Charles V had many problems nearer at hand. The Protestant Reformation had begun, and the Ottoman Turks were striking at North Africa and Vienna. The turbulent *conquistadores,* such as Cortez and Pizarro, seemed likely to forget their loyalty to the king and carve out kingdoms for themselves. Complaints poured in from New Spain, complaints of misgovernment, mistreatment of the Indians, and of disobedience of royal orders. Together they spelled poor administration. What was needed was a governor powerful enough to overawe the unruly conquerors but thoroughly loyal to the king.

Antonio de Mendoza was a logical and wise choice, for he was talented and experienced in affairs of peace and war. He was kindly and humane, and he understood men. Above all, his family had proved its loyalty to generations of monarchs.

On April 17, 1535, Mendoza was named viceroy, governor, and president of the *audiencia,* or court of appeals. He could allow Cortez to continue as captain-general or chief military commander, or assume the duties of commander in chief at his pleasure. He enjoyed, in other words, the authority of the king. His instructions charged him, as the king's representative, to "administer equal justice to all his subjects and vassals, to be active in everything relating to the peace, quiet, prosperity, and extension of the Indies." He was also to aid in the conversion of the Indians to Christianity and to govern well. He had general supervision of the Church.

Mendoza's salary was 3,000 *ducados* as viceroy and governor, an equal amount as president of the *audiencia,* and he also received 2,000 *ducados* annually to maintain a bodyguard. In modern terms his salary was probably equal to about $50,000.

As governor his duties were concerned mainly with the collection of taxes and the payments made out of the royal treasury. This position also required his supervision of mining and similar activities, and of the building of roads and bridges. Though he had not studied law, as president of the *audiencia* he was expected to see that the court's decisions were in keeping with earlier decisions by Spanish courts.

In addition to these charges, Mendoza was given more detailed instructions concerning his relations with the *audiencia* and the Church. As the king's representative, Mendoza was to oversee Church activities, and to aid it in its spiritual mission. He was also commanded to visit all cities and towns to gather information for the purpose of increasing royal revenues. The matter of royal revenues was a theme or undercurrent in all of his duties. Rumors of secret treasure in pagan Indian temples had reached the emperor, and for the benefit of both the non-Christians and the royal treasury, Mendoza was ordered to search these out and seize them in the emperor's name. Possession of great wealth was thought a hindrance to the Indians in becoming good Christians.

The viceroy's duties concerning treatment of the Indians were mentioned frequently in royal orders, but he was cautioned against any rash action that might injure mining. A solution to the complaint that some of the Indians were lazy was to make them work on the royal plantations. The matter of Indian slavery was also to be examined carefully. An unmentioned factor in Indian slavery was that only free Indians paid "tribute" or head tax to the royal treasury. Slavery was not to be encouraged, for the tribute was an important source of revenue.

Mendoza had, furthermore, to examine the defenses of New Spain and particularly of the City of Mexico. He was to make recommendations concerning the building of new forts, the amount of artillery needed, and similar military matters.

The first viceroy arrived in New Spain in 1535. The slow procession from Veracruz to the capital was as ceremonious as if the king himself were present. Mendoza, as first viceroy, was a maker of traditions, and he understood his role thoroughly. Kings of Spain were fortunate when served by able and devoted men such as Antonio de Mendoza. Not all kings appreciated this fact, and many loyal officials were injured because their king believed false charges against them.

The domain over which Mendoza was to preside was not clearly defined, though it included everything from Guatemala north. No one knew what lay beyond the limits of exploration in the "Northern Wonderland." It was the new viceroy's duty to promote exploration.

As chief administrator of this vast area, Mendoza was superb. He paid careful attention to all aspects of his realm, and endeavored faithfully to discharge his numerous duties. He worked late nights and arose early mornings. He concealed any feeling of impatience or irritation, and listened courteously to all who sought audience with him, from the highest-born Spaniard to the humblest Indian.

Mendoza's instructions to his successor reveal the multitude and complexity of the viceroy's problems. The men of New Spain, he warned, were more interested in other people's business than their own. All expected the governor to do as they wished, and the range of requests was truly astonishing. He had learned that the safest policy was to agree with every suggestion, for to disagree quickly caused trouble and accusations. It was best, therefore, to listen patiently to all advice, declare this advice to be excellent, agree to follow it, and then ignore it. If he had followed the advice given him, he said, New Spain would have been in constant turmoil. His principal concern was to avoid sudden changes, especially where Indians were involved. The way to successful government, he added, was to do little and to do it slowly.

Difficulties arose from time to time over the instructions sent by the Council of the Indies in Madrid. New Spain was far away, and the councilors could hardly be expected to find the right solution to every remote and unfamiliar problem. Unwise laws could lead even to revolt, as happened in the 1540's when the "New Laws" abolishing the *encomienda* were put into effect too hastily in Peru. The *encomienda* system was a theoretically humane way of caring for the Indians. Large groups of Indians were "commended" to the care of individual Spaniards, who were responsible for protecting them and bringing them into the Church. In exchange the Indians labored for the *encomenderos*.

Mendoza, sensing the violent resistance these laws would arouse in New Spain, found a solution that many another official would follow in the centuries to come. Ever loyal to the king, Mendoza, with the laws in his hand, said, "I obey but I do not comply."

The viceroy's relations with the *audiencia* could also cause problems, but these Mendoza avoided by his tact. The *audiencia*, though basically a court of appeals, was expected to serve as an advisory council. Like the viceroy, it also had certain legislative authority, especially concerning the Indians. The *audiencia* was expected to serve as a check on the viceroy, but much depended on the characters of the viceroy and the judges. Mendoza maintained cordial relations with the *audiencia*, and it supported him on every major issue. He enlarged its duties and its jurisdiction, especially in lawsuits between Spaniards and natives. He informed his successor that maintaining harmony between the viceroy and the court and among the judges was difficult because the *audiencia*'s duties were not specific. Because the court's decisions were not binding without his signature, he was able to exercise a measure of control over judicial affairs. The *audiencia* also had special rights, and it occasionally served as temporary executive when there was no viceroy.

Increasing royal revenues was a constant problem. Emperor Charles V was involved in wars with France as well as with the Turks in the Mediterranean, and he had borrowed enormous sums from German bankers to finance his election as emperor. His financial needs were always great, but adding to royal revenues was difficult. There was little system in the collecting and accounting for the emperor's monies, and all that Mendoza could tell was that large amounts that belonged in the royal treasury were somehow sidetracked.

By providing account books and requiring sworn statements, Mendoza was able to bring about a marked improvement. Two of the principal sources of royal revenue were the king's fifth of all precious metals found or mined and the tribute paid by the Indians. There were various taxes, fines, and confiscations of property that also went to the royal treasury. Mendoza drew up a set of mining regulations that brought order into the discovery and claiming of mines. He also regulated the process of bringing silver and gold to the mint, so that the king's share could be claimed.

To prevent individuals from stealing the gold or silver once it was collected, Mendoza had strongboxes provided. It required three keys to open these boxes, and the keys were held by three separate officials. No one could get his hands into royal funds without others knowing. These funds, nevertheless, suffered a steady shrinkage. After expenses were met, the balance was shipped to Spain. Here, too, there were great risks, not only from shipwreck but also from English, French, and Dutch corsairs, who hid out among the islands and followed the fleets to board unfortunate stragglers. The greatest blow of all was struck in 1628, when the Dutch West Indies Company squadron seized the entire Spanish treasure fleet off Cuba.

Probably the most crucial issue Mendoza faced was brought about by the "New Laws" and by charges of misrule made against him by Cortez. Father Bartolomé de las Casas was convinced that royal action was needed to save the Indians from total destruction. In 1539 he went to Spain to urge the king to abolish the *encomienda* system. Cortez arrived in Spain the same year, but for a different purpose.

Before the coming of Mendoza as viceroy, Cortez had enjoyed the exclusive right to conduct explorations. This right was taken from him and given to Mendoza. Hoping to regain his former authority, Cortez accused the viceroy of misrule, at the same time that Las Casas was protesting the injuries being done to the Indians. Cortez did not recover his authority, but Las Casas was more successful.

To support his case Las Casas wrote a little book, the *Very Brief Account of the Destruction of the Indies,* in which he made liberal estimates of the number of Indians who had been killed as a result of the Conquest. This lurid account by a Spaniard of his countrymen's misdeeds was speedily translated into English, Dutch, and French. Spain's enemies loved it, and it helped to spread and perpetuate the "Black Legend" of Spanish cruelty.

As a result of the propaganda efforts of Cortez and Las Casas, the Council of the Indies drew up a new Indian code—the "New Laws." Indian slavery was again forbidden, and the *encomienda* was not to be inherited. There were many other restrictions, and if they had been fully put into force the Indians would no longer have been obliged to labor for the Spaniards. The Council sent as *visitador,* or inspector, to New Spain, Francisco Tello de Sandoval. He was authorized to put the "New Laws" into effect, and to investigate the charges Cortez had made against Mendoza. He was given the power to suspend the viceroy if this seemed advisable.

To Sandoval this was the opportunity of a lifetime, and he intended to make the most of it, at Mendoza's expense. For Mendoza it was an exceedingly difficult time. Not only were the *encomenderos* greatly aroused and ready to rebel, but he had to deal with the arrogant and overbearing Sandoval, who did not conceal the fact that he intended to become viceroy. Mendoza persuaded Sandoval to suspend putting the most obnoxious provisions of the "New Laws" into effect, and he rushed off warnings to the king. "All the provisions made . . . ," he wrote, "will not be sufficient remedy; even if his majesty deprived them of their offices and cut off their heads, he could not make them enforce the laws which destroyed his rents and his vassals and depopulated the country. . . ."

Instead of making an impartial investigation of the charges against Mendoza, Sandoval openly sought evidence to prove Mendoza guilty. He might well have succeeded but for the fact that in 1545 Bernaldino de Mendoza, brother of the viceroy, became president of the Council of the Indies. The Council ordered Sandoval to return to Spain. He delayed for two years, but finally had no choice but to comply. He had done nothing worth while.

The Council called Sandoval before it for questioning. His answers were evasive and unsatisfactory, and he was barred from taking any part in considering his own inspection visit to New Spain. The Council also barred him from having a part in any case involving Mendoza. After Mendoza's death his son secured an extension of the prohibition, so that Sandoval could not take part in any case involving Mendoza's children. His humiliation was complete.

After Cortez gave up the struggle for the right to explore, only Pedro de Alvarado remained in the contest against Mendoza. Alvarado was governor of Guatemala, but administration bored him, and in 1538 he received a royal contract to discover and conquer islands in the Pacific Ocean. In 1540 he reached the Pacific coast of New Spain with twelve vessels and six hundred men. He needed supplies, and to obtain these he was obliged to win Mendoza's support.

In November, 1540, Mendoza and Alvarado agreed to share in each other's expeditions. Mendoza had already sent Coronado north in the disappointing search for the mythical Seven Cities. After Coronado withdrew most of the troops from the area north of Mexico City for his expedition, the Mixtec Indians rebelled, and war broke out. Alvarado, who could never pass up a good fight, joined in the fun, and was killed. His death left Mendoza owner of the fleet. Mendoza sent several ships to found a colony in the Philippines, and others to explore the coast of California.

The Mixton War became so serious that Mendoza finally took personal command of the Spanish forces. After he achieved a victory, a new area was opened to the Spanish advance, and it was an area of rich silver deposits. Within a few years Mexican silver mines were producing tremendous quantities of silver ore.

After fifteen years of ruling over a turbulent and extensive land, Mendoza's request for the appointment of a successor was finally granted. Luis de Velasco was named viceroy of New Spain, and he arrived there in 1550. But Mendoza was not allowed to return to Spain, even though he was old and in ill health. In 1551 the king sent him to Lima as viceroy of Peru. This region had been torn by civil war over the "New Laws" in the 1540's, and someone of Mendoza's experience and tact was needed. Mendoza's rule in Peru was far too brief for him to accomplish much. He died in July, 1552.

As the first viceroy, Mendoza set many traditions and precedents that wise viceroys followed. He had pacified the turbulent land, and by kindness, humanity, and patience he had helped the Indians adjust to their new status of vassals of the king of Spain. His practice of devoting one afternoon a week to hearing their complaints had a soothing effect on them, even though he did little more than listen. Four centuries later, presidents such as Porfirio Díaz followed the same policy, and with similar results.

Don Carlos de Sigüenza y Góngora
1645–1700

In the seventeenth century Mexico was in the "Baroque Age," a time of florid ornamentation in writing as well as in architecture. It was a time of superstition and ignorance, when men were convinced that comets were divine warnings of catastrophes to come, a time when students preferred astrology to mathematics. Sigüenza was a misfit in this society; he belonged in the Age of the Enlightenment, but he was a century too soon.

Sigüenza was born in Mexico City in the year 1645, of a family noted in Spain at least from the time of Ferdinand and Isabel. He was a nephew of Don Luis de Góngora y Argote, one of the best-known poets of Spain's Golden Age, who gave his name to a type of obscure poetry, "gongorism," which had many imitators in the seventeenth century. Don Carlos' father had come to Mexico from Spain in the service of one of the viceroys, and he remained in the government for half a century. His chief talent was in handling fiscal accounts. Little is known of Sigüenza's mother, but it was through her that he had the right to add the distinguished surname Góngora to his father's name, Sigüenza.

It seems likely that Don Carlos' early education was conducted by his father, who had been tutor of a Spanish prince, Baltasar Carlos, the son of Philip IV. In 1660 he began his instruction to enter the Society of Jesus. In the Jesuit academy he studied the humanities and excelled in philosophy, literature, and theology. After seven and a half years he was expelled, apparently as a result of inability to submit to the rigid discipline. This was a bitter blow to him, and he tried more than once to win reinstatement without success. Throughout his entire life he felt deeply the fact that he was not a Jesuit.

Don Carlos continued his studies at the University of Mexico, and became skilled in Indian languages. In 1672 he entered competition for the Chair of Astrology and Mathematics in the university. These professorships were given only after a competition among the various candidates. Only one of the men seeking the Chair had earned degrees in mathematics, and he felt that it should go to him. Don Carlos argued confidently that knowledge of the subject was more important than degrees. He was allowed to remain in the competition, and he won the Chair of Astrology and Mathematics with ease. The salary of a professor was small, and Sigüenza was obliged to look for other ways to earn money.

In 1683 he became chaplain of the Hospital del Amor de Dios, which provided him with living quarters.

From the time he was a student, Don Carlos was an active writer. Many of his writings, unfortunately, were never printed because he could not pay for their publication. He was eager for knowledge on any subject, and confident that what other men could learn he could also master. He wrote poetry, and won recognition as a philosopher, mathematician, astronomer, and historian. In all these activities, except writing poetry, he was excellent. Unlike most of his contemporaries, who regarded learning as massive memorization, he was a deep and tireless thinker, a true scholar. His reputation spread far from Mexico, even to the courts of Europe. Louis XIV of France heard of him and offered him a place and a pension at Versailles. He won many honors and titles in Mexico, but as he dryly remarked, they "sound like a great deal but are worth little."

Sigüenza's poetry won little distinction, but his prose was more enduring. Much of his writing was on theological subjects, and he made a sincere and successful effort to live according to Christian principles. He gave of his time and his money to those in need. One man who sought his aid was a Puerto Rican who, because of a series of near calamities, had traveled around the world. Don Carlos was so moved by the story of his troubles that he persuaded the viceroy to aid the man. He also wrote the *Misfortunes of Alonso Ramírez,* a narrative of the Puerto Rican's misadventures, which was published in 1690. The book became a classic adventure story, and may have inspired some later Mexican novels.

Don Carlos became one of the most distinguished men of Mexico City, and his knowledge of so many subjects brought frequent requests for his services. The principal reward for these services was the firm friendship of royal officials from the viceroys down. Occasionally one of them paid for the publication of one of his books, as happened with his *Astronomical and Philosophical Libra.*

One of his intimate friends was the archbishop. Both were intelligent, spirited men, and occasionally their friendly discussions evolved into heated arguments. On one such occasion Don Carlos warned the archbishop to remember whom he was addressing. The archbishop whacked him over the head with his crutch, breaking his glasses and bathing his face in blood. The incident did not injure their warm friendship; in fact, Don Carlos regarded the archbishop as a saint. The archbishop's gifts to the poor were famous throughout Mexico. In sixteen years he gave away some two million pesos. The archbishop's hat was one of Sigüenza's most prized possessions, and he was convinced that any sick person who touched it would be cured of his illness.

Despite his belief in miracles and his efforts to give his research a religious meaning, Don Carlos had only scorn for astrology. He was greatly annoyed that more students were interested in astrology than in his main love, mathematics. The scientist in him spoke when he called astrology "a diabolical invention and, consequently, alien to science, method, principle, and truth. . . ." He was clearly a curious combination of modern, scientific, and medieval outlooks.

In the year 1680 the "Great Comet" appeared, causing fear and apprehension among the superstitious of Europe as well as Mexico. In Mexico only Don Carlos greeted the comet's appearance with curiosity and pleasure. He felt that as Royal Cosmographer it was his duty to explain the phenomenon and to quiet the needless fears of his countrymen. In January, 1681, he presented a pamphlet entitled *Philosophical Manifest Against Comets Stripped of Their Dominion Over the Timid.*

An astounding uproar greeted this mild effort to restore public confidence. From Yucatán came a pamphlet written by Martín de la Torre that, using astrological traditions, attempted to prove that comets were warnings from God of coming disasters. Don Carlos replied with another pamphlet in which he stressed the superiority of science over astrology.

One of his colleagues at the University of Mexico joined the attack with the novel notion that comets were composed of human sweat and the vapors from dead bodies! Don Carlos refused to reply to such obvious foolishness.

The most formidable opposition came from the eminent Austrian Jesuit scholar Father Eusebio Francisco Kino (Kühn). Father Kino had abandoned his academic career to work among the Indians of Sonora and Arizona, where missions he built may still be seen. Kino had observed the Great Comet before leaving Europe, and he wrote a book called *Astronomical Exposition*. Before leaving Mexico City, he gave Don Carlos a copy of the book, suggesting that he might learn something by reading it.

Don Carlos took this as a challenge, and his reply was an important book called *Astronomical and Philosophical Libra*. He was wounded by the fact that Kino did not recognize him as a first-rate mathematician because, as he said, he had not studied at a European university. He was sure that Kino believed that mathematicians might not grow "amidst the reeds and cattails on the margin of a Mexican pond."

Kino supported the belief that comets were warnings of calamities to come, and suggested that anyone with any sense would know it. Sensitive as he was, Don Carlos was deeply offended by the suggestion that he was dull-witted. The fact that Father Kino was an honored member of the Jesuit order, while Don Carlos had repeatedly been denied readmission, could only have added to his sorrow.

In the book that he wrote, Don Carlos showed that he was scientifically far ahead of most of his contemporaries in Europe as well as in Mexico. While most men were still willing to accept traditional explanations for everything, even if these could be proved false, he insisted on proof and demonstration. His attitude was what later came to be called the "scientific approach." "Would it be creditable to the intelligence," he asked, "to accept the teachings of others without looking into the premises on which their ideas are based?" Clearly it would not be.

In the seventeenth century the teachings of the Greek philosopher-scientist Aristotle were still accepted without question or doubt. Since his teachings were accepted and proclaimed by the Church, those who argued against Aristotle's beliefs were regarded as heretics, enemies of the faith. Yet Don Carlos, who had been ordained as a priest, declared that "even Aristotle, the avowed Prince of Philosophers who, for so many centuries, has been accepted with veneration and respect, does not deserve credence . . . when his judgments are opposed to truth and reason. . . ."

By 1693 Don Carlos was in ill-health, and had outlived most of his closest friends. Despite his ill-health he served the viceroy on an important mission. The French were penetrating the Gulf of Mexico, even though La Salle's colony in Texas had been destroyed by Indians. Earlier Spanish attempts to found a settlement at Pensacola Bay had failed. Now a settlement there was necessary to prevent the valuable bay from falling to France. The viceroy sent Don Carlos to explore and map the region and to make recommendations.

After fulfilling this duty, Don Carlos recommended that a settlement be founded immediately. Delay followed delay, and it was not until 1698 that an expedition was sent to Pensacola. A French ship arrived soon afterward, and the Spanish commander immediately abandoned the area and sailed back to Mexico. To excuse his action he declared that Don Carlos's survey was incorrect. Although Don Carlos was obviously too ill to travel, the commander demanded that he make a new survey. The new viceroy, the Count of Montezuma, agreed that Don Carlos should make a new survey or give a reasonable explanation.

Don Carlos agreed to make a new survey, but only on certain conditions. He would stake his library, mathematical instruments, and telescopes, worth more than 3,000 pesos, on the correctness of his first survey. The commander must put up a similar sum.

The viceroy dropped the matter, and sent a new expedition to Pensacola. Don Carlos probably could not have survived the voyage, and the attack on his honor and ability very likely hastened his death. He died on August 22, 1700.

Had Don Carlos lived in Europe, he would have been one of

that small, important group of scholars whose inquiring minds and faith in human reason introduced the Scientific Age and the modern world. In his will he gave his body to science, so that something could be learned of the kidney stones that had so long caused him pain. "I request," he wrote, "that whatever deductions are made shall be revealed to other physicians and surgeons so that they may have data to guide them in administering to other sufferers. I ask in God's name that this be done for the common good, and I command my heir not to interfere. . . ."

Even to the end Don Carlos Sigüenza y Góngora did not abandon either his search for truth and knowledge or his dedication to serving mankind. In the century that followed his death, Mexico as well as Europe moved from an age of fear and superstition to the Age of Reason, to an outlook of self-confidence and optimism. The small world of the searchers for truth such as Don Carlos became the world of Western man. The progress of Western civilization owes much to men like Don Carlos.

José María Morelos
1765–1815

Morelos was a parish priest who became one of Mexico's martyrs of the independence movement.

José María Morelos, one of Mexico's most respected heroes, was born in the city of Valladolid (modern Morelia) on October 4, 1765. After his father died in 1779, Morelos went to live with an uncle in Apatzingán, in tropical southern Mexico. This uncle, Felipe Morelos, owned a *recua,* or mule train, which he used in carrying goods between the Pacific port of Acapulco and Mexico City. Morelos worked as an *arriero,* or mule driver.

In 1790 Morelos entered the College of San Nicolás in Valladolid, to study for the priesthood. It has been said that the vocabulary used by mule drivers is similar to that used by priests and that the step from one to the other was therefore easy. At San Nicolás, Morelos became acquainted with Father Miguel Hidalgo, who was rector of the college. In 1810 Hidalgo launched the Mexican Revolution, to win independence from Spain.

After completing his studies at San Nicolás, Morelos entered the University of Mexico for examinations leading to the degree of Bachelor of Arts. He was sent as *cura*, or parish priest, to the town of Uruapan to teach grammar and rhetoric. This little town is near where the volcano of Paricutín rose in a Tarascan Indian cornfield a century and a half later. In 1798 Morelos was sent to be parish priest in Tamácuaro de la Aguacana, in tropical Mexico. His mother and sister accompanied him, but his mother grew ill from the endless heat, and decided to return to Valladolid. She died on the journey home, and Morelos was soon transferred to the nearby parish of Carácuaro. His request to be moved to a cooler climate was ignored, though he suffered constantly from malaria. The cooler and more pleasant posts were reserved for priests who had been born in Spain. Creole priests were given the less desirable spots. The same was true in political affairs, and this discrimination against the Creoles was one of the reasons they desired independence.

On September 16, 1810, Father Hidalgo assembled the Indians of his parish in the little town of Dolores, and Mexico's struggle for independence began. Hidalgo and other Creoles had planned a revolt for independence to begin during the annual fair at San Juan de los Lagos. But someone informed the viceroy of the conspiracy, and he sent troops to arrest the plotters. Forewarned in time, Hidalgo had to decide between arrest and starting an Indian uprising. He called out to the Indians of his parish, and in so doing began a genuine social revolution quite different from what the Creoles had planned. The Indians, once aroused, were determined to repay all the wrongs they had suffered since the Conquest, and they made no distinction between Spaniards born in Spain and the Creoles.

When Morelos learned of the Hildalgo revolt, the "Grito de Do-lores," he decided to talk with his former teacher and to offer his services as a chaplain in the revolutionary armies. But Hidalgo commissioned him to go to southern Mexico to recruit troops. From this time on, the former parish priest and mule driver was a military commander and a statesman, the foremost spokesman of Mexican liberals.

Hidalgo's career was brief. His uncontrollable Indian hordes swept into Guanajuato and massacred all the Creoles and Span-iards who sought refuge in the town granary. Creoles now had to forget their own plans for independence, and join the royalists in order to save their own lives. Hidalgo's army marched on Mex-ico City, and defeated an army sent to check it. Though the way to Mexico City was then open, Hidalgo turned back, and his army melted away. His reason for this move is not known, though he may not have wanted to see another massacre such as had oc-curred at Guanajuato. He raised another army, but was soundly defeated at Puente de Calderón (Bridge of Calderón), and fled toward Texas. One of his former officers captured him and turned him over to royalists. In July, 1811, he was executed by a firing squad. The Indian attempt at revolution was over.

Morelos, though he had no previous military training, learned the art of war on the battlefield, and became a capable com-mander. He did not raise a mob army as Hidalgo had done, but preferred small, well-trained forces led by carefully chosen offi-cers. For a time he controlled most of southern Mexico.

Although he spent much of his time in the saddle, Morelos suffered constantly from both migraine headaches and malaria. Both of these maladies at times made any effort painful, but he did not flinch from his duty at any time.

Although Hidalgo had raised an Indian *tumulto* where a Creole uprising had been planned, Morelos attracted Indians, Creoles, and mestizos (mixed bloods) to his banner. Unlike Hidalgo, he was able to select able officers and to delegate suitable authority to them. His second in command was another priest, Mariano Matamoros. Another man who rendered valuable services to Morelos and his cause was an American adventurer from Tennessee, Peter Ellis Bean. Bean had entered Spanish Texas in 1800 with Philip Nolan and others on an expedition to catch wild horses along the Brazos River. A Spanish force attacked them, killed Nolan, and captured the others. After a number of years in limited confinement in Chihuahua, Bean was imprisoned in a dungeon in Acapulco. When Morelos reached this area, Bean escaped and joined him. His knowledge of the manufacture of gunpowder was valuable, and he served also as an artillery officer. In 1814 Morelos sent him to New Orleans for aid; he arrived in time to join Jackson's forces in the battle against the British. Soon after this, he learned that Morelos had been captured.

In 1811 Morelos wrote: "Now there is no Spain because the French are in control of it. There is no Ferdinand VII because he went to France voluntarily . . . or he was carried away by force and no longer exists as king. . . ." Later he justified the rebellion by saying: "When kings are absent, sovereignty resides in the nation, which is free to form the type of government it desires. No nation is obliged to remain the slave of another. . . ."

After Hidalgo's capture and execution, Morelos continued his campaigns. While he was trying to get his army in a position to attack the important city of Puebla, General Félix María Calleja captured his base at Zitácuaro. He moved on to besiege Morelos at Cuautla. During the long siege Calleja expressed grudging admiration for Morelos and the defenders. "This priest," he wrote, "is a second Mohammed."

Unlike Hidalgo, Morelos sought no high-sounding titles, nor would he allow them to be attached to his name. He rejected the title of Supreme Highness, which Hidalgo had accepted earlier. The only title he would permit was the more modest "Servant of the Nation." He was never an imposing figure, for he was only a little over five feet in height, and stocky in build. He suffered a number of serious accidents and attempts on his life. Once he was warned that a man with a big belly was coming to kill him. He remained calm. "There is no one here more big-bellied than I am," he said, "and my ailments are wearing me out."

The starving patriots slipped out at night, at the very time Calleja was planning to abandon the siege. The royalists pursued the fleeing soldiers and civilians, and slaughtered them. Families were so badly separated that fifteen years later some of the survivors still did not know what had happened to other relatives during the flight. The patriots' losses were heavy, and most of Morelos's escorts gave their lives that he might escape. A severe blow was the capture of Leonardo Bravo, one of his ablest officers. Bravo was offered his life if he would persuade his brothers to desert Morelos. He ignored this proposal, and was executed.

Calleja returned to Mexico City claiming a great victory over Morelos. As part of the victory celebration a play was presented in which some of the lines lampooned Calleja. A soldier held a turban, saying: "Here is the turban of the Moor I captured." "And where is the Moor?" he was asked. "Unfortunately, he escaped."

The defense of Cuaulta for two months was a heroic effort by Morelos and his men, and it prevented Calleja from ending the war. Morelos spent the next few months recruiting a new army. He badly needed a major victory to boost patriot morale. Puebla was an important prize, but it seemed too well defended for a rapid conquest. Instead, he attacked Oaxaca, with an olive branch in one hand and a sword in the other. The olive branch was spurned with insulting remarks.

The angry patriots swept into the city and looted it. Their triumph was a heartening one, and the rebel cause looked more promising. Morelos was at the peak of his career as a revolutionary leader.

His next goal was the Pacific port of Acapulco, which he had visited frequently in his youth. His determination to take Acapulco was probably his most serious error. He spent seven months besieging the city, and thus gave Calleja time to make preparations to destroy the rebel forces. By the time the city surrendered, the patriot cause was virtually doomed. Calleja raised and equipped Creole forces in all parts of Mexico.

After taking Acapulco, Morelos hurried to Chilpancingo, where a Congress of patriots was assembling to create a government.

Many of the soldiers who fought in the patriot armies still believed they were fighting to defend Mexico against those who would surrender it to Napoleon. Even among the Indians there was still a powerful sentiment of loyalty to the king and a reluctance to oppose him. Patriot leaders such as Morelos often had to disguise their intentions or lose their followers. The Congress of Chilpancingo decided, nevertheless, that the time had come to declare independence. Some leaders protested that this would weaken the cause rather than strengthen it. The majority voted for the declaration, and on November 6, 1813, the Congress declared Mexico independent of Spain.

Immediately after the declaration of independence Morelos set out on a campaign to conquer Valladolid, his own birthplace and that of the revolution. He felt that it should be the seat of the new Congress, the rebel capital. As his troops moved to attack Valladolid, a large body of royalist reinforcements fell on them from the rear. This unexpected blow threw the patriots into confusion.

Morelos and his officers rallied their men and prepared to renew the attack, but their confidence had been shaken and they were expecting defeat. The royalists captured a patriot messenger with an order to patriot troops to blacken their faces, so they could tell friend from foe. With blackened faces a detachment of royalist troops slipped out of the city at night. They threw the patriots into such confusion that they fired at one another and then fled. The campaign had to be abandoned. The defeat at Valladolid was a blow from which the patriots never recovered.

Morelos retreated to the southwest, with royalist troops at his heels. The patriots made a desperate stand, but the royalist artillery was devastating. In this defeat Morelos lost one of his two ablest officers, Mariano Matamoros, who was captured and shot. The retreat continued, but it was becoming a rout, a flight for life. Most of the patriots seemed to feel that their cause was doomed. The Congress relieved Morelos of his military duties.

In March of 1814 Ferdinand VII was released by Napoleon, and he returned to the Spanish throne. Men who had fought in his name, believing they were really opposing the French, would no longer resist his armies. His return to Madrid was the final blow.

As the insurgent cause sank toward its nadir, the various leaders began quarreling bitterly among themselves. Viceroy Calleja, hoping to crush the last spark of the rebellion, offered generous terms to those who surrendered, and threatened with death those who did not accept. Morelos regarded the offer as a trick, and did not nibble at the bait. Hundreds of patriots accepted the offer.

Morelos was convinced that a constitution was necessary to save the revolutionary cause. A constitution would raise the patriots in the eyes of foreign governments and also help unite the patriots, who were quarreling among themselves. It was Carlos María Bustamente who convinced him that a constitution was absolutely vital. Mexico "cannot be free," he declared, "as long as the provinces do not support this idea; foreign powers cannot recognize us as long as an august body where sovereignty may be deposited is missing. . . ."

The Congress had spent most of its days on the move, and no constitution could be written in the saddle. It finally found refuge in the remote village of Apatzingán. In a solemn ceremony the members of the Congress swore allegiance to the constitution, embraced one another, and danced for joy. Morelos, who was a deputy in the Congress, joined in the celebration. He had arrived at Apatzingán about the time the Congress was completing its work, and he had little to do with preparing the constitution. He believed that a strong president was necessary, but the constitution provided for a weak three-man executive and a powerful legislature. Morelos signed the constitution nevertheless, saying that he considered it impractical but probably all that could be hoped for under the circumstances.

The constitution did raise the patriots' spirits and enhance their respect abroad, for it demonstrated their determination to continue the one-sided struggle. Calleja was thoroughly aroused by it. The Inquisition, which Ferdinand VII had re-established, called those who supported the constitution atheists, heretics, and enemies of the Church. Their heresy was political rather than religious, however, for the constitution declared the Catholic faith to be the official religion.

The Congress elected three men to serve as the chief executive: Morelos, José María Cos, and José María Liceaga. Once more its sessions were to be mainly on horseback, for royalist forces pursued it relentlessly, determined to destroy it. Cos rebelled against the Congress that had elected him, and tried to overthrow it. The Congress sent Morelos to crush the rebellion. When Morelos appeared, Cos found himself deserted and alone, and he had no choice but to surrender. Such divisions and feuds among the patriots greatly weakened them and made Calleja's work easier.

Protecting the patriot Congress now became the most crucial problem, for the royalist pressure increased. The leaders decided on a daring journey through royalist territory to the east coast of Mexico, where they might receive the expected aid from the United States. Morelos was given the difficult task of escorting the Congress on its perilous journey. He had about a thousand men in his command, but only half of them had guns. His tricks deceived Calleja for a time as to the route and destination of the Congress, but there were many royalist columns in the field. One of these happened across Morelos's trail, and followed it rapidly.

Outnumbered and surprised, the patriots hastily prepared for battle while the Congress escaped. In two fierce charges the royalists broke through the patriot lines. "Go save the Congress," Morelos ordered Nicolás Bravo; "it matters not if I perish." In this he was wrong, for he was the principal prize.

Morelos rode for a steep hill, but as he dismounted a squad of royalist soldiers surrounded him. Their officer was Lieutenant Matías Carranco, a former patriot. "Señor Carranco," said Morelos as he surrendered, "it appears that we know each other."

The Congress escaped, but the Hidalgo-Morelos revolution was over. Morelos was taken to Tenango and forced to watch while twenty-seven of his comrades were shot by royalist firing squads. On November 22nd he reached Mexico City. Even before he arrived, the army, the Church, and the Inquisition were arguing over which of them should hold the prisoner's trial. In the end all of them took part in the trial, which began the same day Morelos arrived.

Morelos was accused of treason, of disloyalty to the king, and of promoting independence. He replied that since there had been no king of Spain when he joined the movement, he had not committed treason by working for independence. He was assigned a lawyer. This reluctant individual denounced the revolution but expressed the mild hope that Morelos would be pardoned. He spent the rest of his time apologizing for the fact that he had been put in such an embarrassing position. He had been given only three hours to prepare his case, but since he judged his client guilty, this was more time than he needed.

Early on the morning of December 22nd Morelos was placed in a coach and taken from Mexico City along the road toward the shrine of Guadalupe. He knew this was his last journey, but he had no way of knowing the final destination. When the coach stopped at the village of San Cristóbal Ecatépec, Morelos knew by the expressions on the faces of his guards that this was the place of execution. Calleja was afraid a riot would break out if the sentence were carried out publicly in Mexico City. Morelos was still a popular hero.

The commander of the troops at San Cristóbal had not been informed of his unpleasant duty, and was unprepared for it. Morelos was placed in a storeroom to wait. The village priest joined him, and together they knelt in prayer. Outside the window they heard the sound of marching men, and an officer giving hasty instructions to the firing squad. Morelos paused for a moment, and listened. Soldiers entered the room and tied his arms to his sides. One of them placed a blindfold over his eyes, then led him to the courtyard. "Put him on his knees there," the officer ordered, indicating the spot with his sword. Morelos, his legs still heavily shackled, knelt and made his final prayer.

"Lord, thou knowest if I have done well," he intoned; "If ill, I implore thy infinite mercy." The officer gave orders; the soldiers raised muskets to their shoulders, and fired. Morelos fell forward.

In 1823, after Mexican independence had been won, Morelos's

remains were removed to Mexico City, to be placed with those of other heroes of the struggle. Later these remains of the leaders were placed in a sepulcher under the monument dedicated to the revolutionary heroes on the Paseo de la Reforma. It seems unlikely that Morelos's remains were among those placed under the monument, however, for friends had moved them to a secret grave. No one knows where it is.

Morelos has been recognized as one of Mexico's principal heroes of all time. In 1828 his birthplace, Valladolid, was renamed Morelia in his honor, and in 1862 the State of Morelos was created. Even more important, perhaps, is the fact that what Morelos desired for Mexico became the goal of Mexican liberals from his time onward. Many of these goals have been achieved; none of them has been forgotten. His sacrifices were not in vain.

Manuel Abad y Queipo
1751–1825

Abad's principal service was in the Mexican province of Michoacán, where he was bishop when the movement for independence began. His people knew him as a great humanitarian. He tried to retain Mexican loyalty to Ferdinand VII, but Ferdinand was not grateful.

The birthplace of Abad y Queipo was the town of Villarpedre, near Oviedo in the Spanish province of Asturias. His ancestors had lived in this part of northern Spain since before the Arab conquests of 711, and the castle of Abad was one of the principal refuges from Arab raids. Members of the family served as officials and judges, and were distinguished by their loyal service to many kings.

Although Abad was of illegitimate birth, his father sent him to complete his education at the ancient University of Salamanca. He earned degrees in law and canon law. After he was ordained as a priest, he accompanied Archbishop Cayetano Francos y Monroy to the city of Comayagua in Guatemala.

In 1779 the archbishop appointed Abad as attorney general for the Church in Guatemala. He was also named lawyer for the royal *audiencia*. He served ably both king and Church, and earned a reputation for fairness. The climate of Guatemala did not agree with him, however, and in 1784 he accompanied Bishop Antonio de San Miguel to Michoacán in New Spain. In Valladolid, modern Morelia, in the Mexican state of Michoacán, Abad was given financial duties for the Church, and he also served as a judge in the Church court.

As Abad's prestige grew, he was named sacristan of León and of Guanajuato. He delegated his duties in those towns to others, for he was needed in Valladolid to perform more important functions. His interest in education led him to present a plan for university reform similar to the reforms then being introduced in Spanish universities. At his own expense he hired a mathematician to teach in two of the seminaries of Valladolid. Like many other priests, Abad had caught the spirit of the Enlightenment, and he wanted to see education lifted from the narrow confines of the past.

Smallpox epidemics occasionally struck Valladolid and other cities in New Spain. In 1804 Abad had vaccine brought to the city even before the royal vaccinating expedition from Spain arrived. He urged the people to take advantage of the opportunity for vaccination. This was at a time when many countries of Europe still had not accepted vaccination as a means of preventing smallpox epidemics.

In June, 1805, Abad won the competition for the office of penitentiary canon of the cathedral church of Valladolid. This was an important position, and it represented another step up the ladder.

Abad was deeply concerned over the welfare of the poor, and he was convinced that the Indian tribute should be abolished. This tribute was not only a burden on all Indian men; it also marked them as being at the bottom of the social scale. From 1791 on, Abad repeatedly urged abolition of the unfair tax. In 1810 Spain finally ended the tribute in all parts of Spanish America, though it was restored by some of the former colonies after independence. For his efforts in behalf of the downtrodden, Abad earned the title of "Father of the Poor."

Public welfare, Abad believed, would be greatly served by the improvement of agriculture and the breakup of the enormous estates into small farms. In this he anticipated one of the agrarian reforms consistently demanded in the twentieth century. The large landowners, then as now, resisted this proposed reform.

The need for improvement in commerce also concerned Abad. "Why," he asked, "is our flour of Puebla not able to compete in Havana with that of the United States?" He pointed out that laborers in the United States were paid wages double those paid men in Puebla. The flour from Puebla did not have to be shipped such a great distance to reach a port, and the voyage from Veracruz to Havana was much shorter than that from Philadelphia or New York. Flour from Puebla paid no duty, but that from the United States paid a heavy impost. Despite these advantages, the Mexican flour cost a peso per barrel more than that from the United States. Abad attributed this to the numerous obstacles to commerce, and to the fact that Mexican merchants had to rely on foreign capital borrowed at high interest rates. Other Spaniards had occasionally made similar observations about Spanish commerce, but little was ever done to improve it.

In 1809 Bishop Marcos Mariana of Michoacán appointed Abad as provisor and vicar general of the diocese. In July of the same year the bishop died. Abad's name was immediately proposed as a candidate for the vacant benefice. From many directions and many people came enthusiastic letters in support of his candidacy. In February, 1810, the Council of the Indies named him Bishop of Michoacán.

At the same time that Abad assumed his new duties, the Hidalgo-Morelos revolt began. Ever loyal to Spain, Abad opposed this rebellion in every way possible. Because of his strong loyalist feelings, he approved the action of a group of Spaniards who deposed the viceroy on the grounds that he sympathized with the Creoles. It was this illegal act, however, that began a whole series of unlawful moves Abad could not regard as satisfactory. Like many other Spaniards, he was blinded by a powerful sense of loyalty to the king that was almost a religious conviction.

In 1808, when the Spanish resistance to Napoleon began, Abad recommended that all the silver vessels in the churches be contributed to the war chest. He also thought that priests should discontinue carrying out pious works except in primary education and the operation of hospitals. Every resource available should be devoted to the conduct of the war against the French.

With regard to the struggle for independence in New Spain, Abad's position was less clear-cut, at least to many of his contemporaries. He had frequently expressed sympathy with the Creoles, and had requested some adjustments in their behalf. He could not, however, find any grounds to justify their rebellion, even though their pleas for reforms as well as his own had been ignored. He regarded protests as proper, for these did not imply disloyalty to the king, but rebellion was a far different matter.

In 1809 Abad wrote to the viceregal council in Mexico City urging an increase in the military forces of the kingdom. He was convinced that the existing troops were not strong enough to defend the land against Napoleon. He stressed the need for manufacturing arms and equipment, pointing out that poorly armed soldiers could not be effective. The council courteously thanked him for his report, then laid it aside. Abad wrote to Spain in the same year, warning that Spanish Americans in all parts of the empire desired independence.

In 1811 Hidalgo was captured and executed, but the rebellion continued under Morelos and other leaders. Morelos came much closer to success than had Hidalgo. Some Spaniards suspected Abad of secretly favoring the rebels, while the rebels considered him a major enemy to their cause. When elections were held for representatives to be sent to the Cortes, or assembly, in Spain, Veracruz, Querétaro, and other cities chose him even though he

Don Carlos de Sigüenza y Góngora (1645-1700) Mathematician, astronomer, cartographer, and poet. Mexico's greatest colonial scholar.

José Mariá Morelos (1765-1815) the parish priest who became Mexico's greatest fighter for independence.

Antônio Vieira, S. J. (1608-1697)
Brazil's great missionary-priest and protector
Indians.

*José Bonifacio de Andräda
(1763-1838)* Brazil's greatest colonial
scientist and "Architect of Independence."

*Cândido Mariano de Silva Rondon
(1865-1958)* Founder of the Indian Protective Society and friend of the Indian.

was not a Creole, but he did not go to Spain at the time. He wrote to rebel leaders offering them pardons if they surrendered, but they suspected a trap and declined the offer. Morelos, whom Abad had excommunicated, accused him of causing unnecessary bloodshed. Other priests who supported the rebel cause were equally bitter against him.

The exchange of letters and accusations between Abad and the rebel priests was heated and violent in language. Abad actually favored reforms, even some of those Morelos proposed. It was simply his profound sense of devotion to the king that prevented him from seeing any justice in the rebel cause.

"Our insurgents," he declared, "were criminals and delinquents at the beginning of the insurrection. It follows that they are criminals of high treason . . . and that they ought to be classified as . . . assassins, thieves, . . . and perjurers, . . . especially the priests on account of their better instruction and the holiness of their ministry. . . ."

The rebels frequently pointed out what the former English colonies had accomplished. Abad declared that they did not understand the differences between the English and the Spanish colonies. In pointing out these differences in legal, political, and cultural traditions, he showed a rather surprising knowledge of Anglo-America and the American Revolution. It was too soon, he felt, to determine whether or not the English colonies had been damaged or improved by gaining independence.

When Abad had been named bishop-elect of Michoacán, the Napoleonic Wars prevented him from receiving confirmation from the Pope. Both the rebels, to whom he was a dangerous foe, and the conservative royalists, who resented his support of reforms, used this lack of papal confirmation as grounds for attacking his position.

Ferdinand VII returned to the Spanish throne in 1814, after Napoleon released him from confinement in Bayonne. Ferdinand had been reared to be an absolute monarch, and he never wavered in his loathing of constitutions and all things of a liberal character. As soon as possible he threw out the Spanish Constitution of 1812, and began to persecute the Spanish liberals who had fought the French to preserve his throne for him. Many Spaniards, such as Abad, who had remained completely loyal to Ferdinand, now found that he had little gratitude for anyone's sacrifices. Abad was stunned to learn that Ferdinand had appointed another priest as bishop in his place.

Abad immediately wrote to the king, requesting that he not be replaced. Ferdinand ordered him to come to Spain. His appointment as bishop was still not confirmed by king or Pope. His trip to Veracruz was slow and often interrupted, for rebel bands still held much of southern Mexico, and to them Abad was a prize worth taking. He finally reached Spain in 1815. In June of that year his successor wrote the king, asking to be relieved of his duties, for he lacked the strength to carry them out.

When Abad met the king all seemed to be well for him, for Ferdinand appeared to be much impressed with his intelligence, and appointed him attorney general. Three days later, however, another blow fell, for he received a blunt message which said: "The king our Lord has been pleased to decide that your Excellency shall not be attorney general because his Majesty has learned that your Excellency has a case pending in the Tribunal of the Holy Inquisition."

The case concerning his appointment as bishop was heard first, and it was decided that his appointment was proper and legal and that there was no need for the king to approve it. This was only a partial solution to the matter, however, for nothing was said about restoring him to the bishopric of Michoacán. The pending case before the Inquisition, furthermore, was to cause him added grief.

During his arguments with rebel priests, and in particular with Dr. José María Cos, Abad had freely expressed the opinions of the great European philosophers. The Carmelite priests of Valladolid, who were apparently envious of his prestige, denounced him to the Inquisition on the grounds that his faith was suspect. He had, obviously, read dangerous books, works that were prohibited. In 1813, nearly three years before the case came before the Holy Tribunal of Madrid, the Cortes had abolished the Inquisition of Mexico. In 1814, after Ferdinand was restored to his throne, he had re-established the Inquisition.

Though the Inquisition of Mexico never recovered its former position, one member tried to revive its prestige by getting together a case against Abad. But it was a useless effort, for the most that he could do was to accuse Abad of laxness because he had excused a priest from attending the choir. He was also accused of having read a prohibited book and of praising the government of the United States. These alleged acts were presented as "proof" that he was a heretic and that, whether guilty or not, he deserved punishment.

What actually caused the charges against Abad was the fact that he was a Gachupín, or Spaniard born in Spain. These Peninsulares enjoyed a monopoly of the positions of power in the Church as well as in civil administration, a fact that was greatly resented by the Creoles. The Peninsulares owed their privileged position to the king, and this was a powerful motive for their great loyalty to him. It was also a reason for their bitter opposition to the independence movements. Abad, though loyal to the king, had seen some merit in the complaints of the Creoles.

In March, 1816, the Inquisition summoned Abad to appear before it. He protested that, as bishop-elect, he had the right to be tried only by the Pope. He refused to appear. The Inquisition threatened to use force unless he appeared voluntarily. Abad appealed to the king, but Ferdinand did not reply. Once more the Inquisition demanded that he appear in its chambers.

Bailiffs from the Holy Office arrested Abad and confined him in the Dominican convent of Rosario. He still refused to recognize the Inquisition's right to try him. The arguments went on and on. Abad's lawyer appealed to the king. He mentioned Abad's loyal service, his sixty-five years of age, his ill-health, and the harshness of his confinement.

From Mexico, too, came many pleas for Abad and protests against his arrest and imprisonment. Some letters pointed out that he had worked loyally and successfully against the Hidalgo-

Morelos rebels. Others pointed out that Abad's fate was causing great discouragement among those who had remained loyal to the king. Abad's treatment was a poor reward for loyalty.

Finally, in order to save face, the inquisitor-general urged Abad to submit to its jurisdiction on the promise that he would be exonerated. After consulting his friends, Abad agreed, asking that the Holy Office conclude its proceedings quickly. This request was ignored, though eventually Abad was completely exonerated.

Not yet thoroughly satisfied, Abad requested the king to order the Council of State to consider the charges made against him. The Council examined several of the points on which there had been some doubt, and decided in his favor. The king declared the case against him null and void. His innocence was now fully acknowledged, and he was restored to his post as bishop of Michoacán, though he never returned there.

Abad remained in Madrid, increasingly shocked at the tyrannical acts of Ferdinand VII. The harsh suppression of liberties turned former supporters against him in Spain as well as in Mexico. Masons and liberals plotted to restore the Constitution of 1812. On January 1, 1820, troops preparing to embark for the colonial wars rebelled. Led by Colonel Rafael Riego, they demanded that Ferdinand restore the Constitution. Ferdinand, frightened at this show of force, and perhaps thinking of the French Revolution, submitted meekly to the demand and promised to rule according to the Constitution.

The end of the absolute monarchy brought Abad out of his seclusion, for he was appointed to the provisional junta formed to see that the king ruled constitutionally. Later he was elected deputy to the Cortes from his native province of Asturias.

The Cortes split into two factions, one radical and the other moderate. This division gave Ferdinand and the absolutists an opportunity to spread confusion and create anarchy. As this anarchy spread, Ferdinand secretly appealed to the monarchs of France, Prussia, and Russia for aid, declaring that he was a prisoner in his own kingdom.

Remembering the French Revolution and the fate of Louis and

Marie Antoinette, the kings of the three countries heeded Ferdinand's appeals. In 1823 France sent an army into Spain. The divided liberals were easily crushed, and Ferdinand became absolute monarch once more. Little remained of his once-enormous empire, and he was soon to lose most of what was tenuously held. It has been said of the Bourbons that they learned nothing and forgot nothing, and Ferdinand was a thorough Bourbon. His rule became more tyrannical than ever.

Because Abad had served on the provisional junta, Ferdinand regarded him as an enemy. He offered Abad a bishopric in Spain, so that he would resign as bishop of Michoacán. Abad fell for this bait, and resigned the bishopric of Michoacán. In the meantime Ferdinand had secretly asked the Pope to withhold confirmation of the Spanish bishopric. As a result, Abad was left with no position or protection after his resignation was accepted.

On May 23, 1824, Abad read in the official gazette a royal decree of pardon for the rebels of 1820. The names of the members of the provisional junta were not included. Two days later, officials came to arrest him.

Abad's "crime" was having served on the provisional junta. He was sentenced to six years' confinement in the convent of Sisla near Toledo, though he was now seventy-four years old, and completely deaf. In January of 1825 he wrote a plea to the king for his release, pointing out that his ill-health would prevent him from living out his term of confinement. The monarch he had served so long and faithfully coldly rejected the pathetic plea.

On September 15, 1825, Abad y Queipo died, having served less than one of his six years of imprisonment. His long career had seen much gratifying service in Guatemala and Michoacán, and many men remembered him with affection and respect. He had been, however, concerned with reforming the colonial régime without breaking up the empire. For this he incurred the wrath of both the rebels and the absolutist king, who abhorred any idea of reform and who had no feeling of gratitude to faithful subordinates. History has raised the name of Abad y Queipo far above that of his fickle and tyrannical master.

PART II

Protectors of the Brazilian Indians

Father Vieira, José Bonifácio, and Cândido Rondon span three centuries of Brazilian history. They had in common a conviction that the Indians were rational beings and should be treated humanely. All were anxious to see the Indians brought fully into Brazilian life. Of these men, only Rondon, who was part Indian, was able to devote most of his time and energy to this cause. Vieira lived in Brazil during the beginning of the Dutch occupation from the 1630's to 1654. In 1640 Portugal freed herself from Spanish rule, and Vieira moved to Lisbon, where he became one of the king's most trusted counselors. Later he was placed in charge of the missions of Maranhão, but the hostility of the slave-owning planters defeated his efforts to protect the Indians.

José Bonifácio never worked directly with Indians, but he made his views known to Brazilians after they had become independent of Portugal. He lived in Portugal for nearly half of his life, then returned to become the "Architect of Brazilian Independence." He was convinced that Brazil could not truly become a nation until all elements of her population were drawn fully into national life. He insisted that the Indians be given the opportunity to become useful citizens. He also demanded the end of Negro slavery. Emancipation came only in 1888, and soon after this, Rondon took up the cause of the Indians. Rondon often acknowledged his indebtedness to the ideas of José Bonifácio.

Antônio Vieira
1608–1697

Father Vieira lived much of his life in seventeenth-century Brazil, during the "Spanish Captivity" (1580–1640), when the kings of Spain ruled Portugal, and during part of the Dutch occupation, 1630–1654. His main interest was the welfare of the Indians, and on this subject he was most eloquent.

Antônio Vieira was born in Lisbon on February 6, 1608. His paternal grandmother was a mulatto serving-woman in the household of a noble family, and his mother's father was an armorer. When Vieira was six, the family moved to Brazil, for his father had been appointed secretary to the court in the Brazilian colonial capital, Bahia.

In Bahia, Vieira studied in the Jesuit academy, where he was a brilliant student. When he was fifteen he entered the Jesuit order as a novice, and later took holy orders. In 1624 he was present when the Dutch West India Company squadron sailed into Bahia and captured the city. Vieira wrote the most detailed account of this Dutch invasion and of the counterattack which forced the Dutch to retreat.

The next few years Vieira was in Olinda, where he lectured on rhetoric at the Jesuit academy. In 1635 he was ordained. By this time the Dutch occupation of Pernambuco had begun. In 1638 he was in Bahia when the Dutch attacked the city again. Vieira made a stirring speech, urging the Brazilians to resist. Again the Dutch failed to complete their conquest of Bahia, and Vieira was chosen to deliver the victory sermon.

In 1640 the Portuguese declared their independence of Spain and named the Duke of Braganza King João IV. Vieira and several Brazilians sailed to Lisbon during the next year to congratulate the king, and to assure him of Brazilian loyalty. Portugal's position was critical, for it seemed likely that Spain would attack. At the same time the Dutch, who had already looted Portugal's Oriental empire, were seizing Portuguese possessions in Africa as well as the northeastern coast of Brazil. Portugal was too weak to resist either enemy, but Spain was the main threat to the homeland.

England, Portugal's traditional ally, was torn by the Puritan revolt, and unable to help against either enemy. The Dutch would have been logical allies against Spain except for their hunger for Portuguese possessions overseas. The Dutch had only recently won their independence from Spain, and they were willing to fight Spain again. They would do so, but for a price—the sugar-plantation region of Brazil and the slave-trading posts of Africa.

The Portuguese king, Dom João IV, was much impressed by Vieira's intelligence and eloquence, and appointed him court preacher. He also made Vieira a trusted adviser. In 1646 he sent Vieira to Holland and France to negotiate with the Dutch over the Brazilian province of Pernambuco. Vieira had a keen awareness of what the Dutch might do, and of the urgency of their demands. He did not agree to the Dutch demands that Portugal cede Pernambuco, but he avoided arousing them to action.

It was in his behind-the-scenes advice to the king rather than in direct diplomacy that Vieira's value was greatest. He knew when Dutch patience was wearing thin, and when it was necessary to yield some point to ease the tension between the two countries. Fortunately for Portugal, the Dutch were sure that time was running in their favor, and they were in no hurry to conclude negotiations. Vieira was equally sure that every delay was advantageous to Portugal, and his view was correct.

Vieira took a long-range view of the struggle with Holland, and did not worry about temporary embarrassments. Early in 1649 he wrote his Papel Forte (strong paper) in which he pointed out that Portugal had no choice but to avoid war with Holland, regardless of the cost. He pointed out that France, the strongest nation in Europe, was careful to avoid war with Spain and Holland at the same time. Portugal, the weakest nation in Europe, was threatened by attacks from Spain and Holland at a time when she needed Dutch aid against Spain.

Many Portuguese regarded Vieira's attitude as unpatriotic, and talked wildly of fighting both Spain and Holland at once. The king kept Portugal out of war with Holland, and ordered the building of warships. At the same time, he sought aid from England and France.

Portugal's trade with Brazil was vital to her economy, and the Dutch West India Company squadrons captured every Portuguese ship they met on the seas. Vieira proposed to solve this problem by creating a chartered trading company like those of England and Holland. He insisted that New Christians (converts from Judaism) and Portuguese Jews, who lived in other European countries, be given guarantees of protection against the Inquisition so that they would be willing to give their financial support to the company. The Inquisition protested, but the situation was so critical that the king authorized the formation of the Brazil Company under Vieira's terms. The Inquisition never forgave Vieira.

The tide began to turn in favor of Portugal when the Anglo-Dutch naval wars began. Holland was overextended and saw the need for concentrating her efforts on defending the valuable possessions she had taken from Portugal in the Orient. Another ally appeared when young Louis XIV came to power in France. To France as well as England, Holland was a serious rival, and both took up the cause of Portugal. Neither country offered direct aid to Brazil, and the Brazilians were obliged to win back their lands from the Dutch by their own efforts. Even when there was no official encouragement from Portugal, they kept up the deadly guerrilla warfare, and made the war painfully costly for the

Dutch West India Company. In 1654 the Dutch abandoned their last posts in Brazil.

Even before the danger from Holland was over, Vieira persuaded the king to send him among the Brazilian Indians. He arrived in Maranhão at the same time a royal edict ordered all Indian slaves freed. Many colonists blamed Vieira for this, to them, obnoxious decree, and his moving sermons against Indian slavery convinced them that he was responsible. He predicted a gloomy future for those men who illegally held Indian slaves.

The colonists assembled, shouting, "Away with the Jesuits!" but they were not yet roused to violence. Vieira wrote a long account of the situation, and sent it to the king. He described the miserable condition of the Indians, even those who were supposed to be free. He asked that the governors be prohibited from using Indians in raising crops, for they abused free Indians as well as slaves.

The settlers of Maranhão were aware of Vieira's influence at the court, and they sent agents to plead their case before the king. They were poor, and they could not afford to buy slaves from Africa. They had no choice but to use Indian labor, and free Indians were reluctant to work. Compulsion was necessary. Their pleas made sense to the king and he sought to achieve a compromise that would satisfy Vieira as well as the planters. He permitted the planters to enslave Indians under certain conditions. Slaves could be taken only in specified areas, and a priest had to pass on the legality of each enslavement. The planters were better satisfied with this law than was Vieira, for he was opposed to Indian slavery for any reason.

Vieira emphasized the reasons for his attitude when he wrote of Indians who had been on friendly terms with the Dutch. "They have conceived such a hatred of the Portuguese nation," he said, "that they wish to have neither peace nor trade with us. . . ." He mentioned others, who were attached to the Dutch through trade and friendship. "In this way the politicos of Holland knew how to purchase the good will and submission of these people," he said, "and transfer them from our obedience to their own. We could have stopped this by the same means, at much less cost, but through not giving a little voluntarily we end by losing everything involuntarily."

In June, 1654, Vieira sailed for Lisbon, to inform the king of the condition of the Indians. Agents representing the planters of Belém and São Luis were already at court, trying to protect their interests. In an effort to improve the administration of Pará and Maranhão, the king had united the provinces under a single governor. When he had asked Vieira if it would be better to have one or two governors, the reply had been, "One honest man is easier to find than two."

The king was troubled by the conflicting requests, and uncertain as to the proper course. He called together a group of priests and asked for their opinion. Their suggestions were incorporated in the law of April, 1655. This law prohibited capture and enslavement of Indians except under specified conditions. Those captives taken in a "just" war (one authorized by the king) could be enslaved. Indians who resisted and obstructed teaching of the gospel were also subject to enslavement. And, finally, Indian captives rescued from cannibals were also eligible for slavery.

The same law also regulated the labor of free Indians, and prohibited the governors from engaging in cultivation. In 1655, the year the law was issued, Vieira was named Superior of the Missions of Maranhão, and given wide authority in all matters concerning the Indians. He traveled to Maranhão with the new governor, who was to put the law into effect. They found the planters angry and resentful, on the verge of rebellion.

In some outlying districts the planters drove the Jesuit missionaries away. The governor dealt firmly with these rebels. He marched in at the head of a body of troops, overawed the planters, and restored the missionaries.

In 1656 Dom João IV died, leaving Vieira with no powerful friend at court. The governor was replaced by a man who was not concerned about Indian slavery. Vieira spent the next five years largely in travels and explorations, to learn all that he could of the many unknown Amazon tribes. Even though he was away much of the time, the planters' resentment continued to grow. In 1661 they expelled all Jesuits from the province and sent them to Lisbon.

Vieira hoped to recover the lost ground, but he was on the losing side in a struggle for power at court. In 1662 a palace revolt deposed the queen-regent, and her son, Alfonso VI, became king in his own right. Because Vieira had supported Prince Pedro against his brother, Alfonso banished him from the court.

Once Vieira was without a royal protector, the Holy Office of the Inquisition seized him. The Inquisition had been suspicious of Vieira for many years because some of his views were unorthodox. The Inquisition had been especially aroused over his insistence on toleration for New Christians. Now there was an opportunity to embarrass and injure him. The Inquisitors moved with deliberate slowness, to drag the proceedings out as long as possible. Vieira remained in prison from 1663 to 1667. At the conclusion of his trial, though no crime had been proved, he was deprived of his license to preach, and ordered to be confined in a monastery.

Fortunately for Vieira, Dom Alfonso was deposed by another palace revolt, and Dom Pedro became prince-regent. Pedro quickly ordered Vieira's release, but would do little else for him. In August, 1669, Vieira went to Rome, to plead the cause of the New Christians, who were still suspected by the Inquisition and occasionally persecuted. Though the Inquisitors of Portugal were aroused by his actions, he did not achieve much success. The Pope gave him a safe-conduct to protect him against future interference by the Portuguese Holy Office. He remained in Rome until 1675, and was one of the most popular preachers in the city.

He left once more for Lisbon, where he tried to interest Dom Pedro in improving the condition of the Brazilian Indians, but with little success. In 1681 he gave up the struggle, and sailed for Brazil. He spent the last sixteen years of his life working in behalf of the Indians.

Vieira's life had been one of many achievements. He won lasting fame for his sermons, which are still regarded as among the best examples of Portuguese prose ever written. He was a valued and effective adviser to the king during the struggles with Holland. He was an explorer and missionary in the Amazon Valley. His main goal was to bring the Indians fully into Brazilian life, and though he never achieved it, others would take up the cause in later centuries.

José Bonifácio de Andrada
1763–1838

The Andradas were an old Portuguese family of Minho and Trás-os-Montes. José Bonifácio's father was a merchant in Santos, today the second maritime city of Brazil but then a sleepy colonial town. The family had come to Brazil near the end of the seventeenth century, and had accumulated a substantial fortune. The family was large, for José Bonifácio had five brothers and four sisters. Even as a boy he displayed signs of exceptional intelligence, though educational facilities were poor throughout colonial Brazil. Most of his early instruction was given him by his parents.

To continue his education, José Bonifácio was sent inland to São Paulo, capital of the captaincy, or province, where a bishop conducted a school that provided courses in logic, metaphysics, rhetoric, and French. The bishop quickly recognized José Bonifácio's intellectual capacities, and predicted a brilliant future for him.

After the expulsion of the Jesuits in 1759, there were no institutions of advanced study in Brazil. Young Brazilians who wished university degrees were obliged to go to Europe, principally to Coimbra in Portugal, but also to Montpellier in France. In 1783

José Bonifácio sailed for Europe, and began the study of law at Coimbra. He was not to see his father again, for his father died in 1789. He did not see his mother again for thirty-six years.

When José Bonifácio began his studies at Coimbra there were twenty-two other Brazilian youths there. The university had been recently reformed by the Marquis of Pombal, who tried to remove all Jesuit influence. Portugal had lived in intellectual isolation from the rest of Europe, according to Pombal, and he wished to see it move into the mainstream. For this reason Pombal sought to introduce the scientific studies that were becoming popular elsewhere in Europe.

José Bonifácio often expressed his feelings in verse, and some of his poems from his student days indicate that he was an avid reader of French and English authors such as Rousseau, Voltaire, Montesquieu, Locke, and Pope. One of his verses proclaimed the success of the English colonies in winning their independence. Reflecting the books he read, José Bonifácio became an enemy of despotism and intolerance, and a devotee of liberty. He became imbued with the optimistic sentiments of the Enlightenment, which held that man was a rational being who could be happy in a society organized on rational bases.

In 1787 José Bonifácio completed his studies of philosophy, and a year later he finished the law course. Instead of returning to Brazil, he went to Lisbon, where relatives arranged for his admission into the Academy of Sciences. In 1790 the Portuguese government commissioned him and two other young men to make a scientific excursion through Europe, at the government's expense. The government was particularly anxious for them to study mineralogy, and to learn the most modern mining techniques. The first stop was Paris, where they were instructed to pursue the complete course of chemistry of M. Fourcroy and the course of mineralogy conducted by M. Le Sage. Paris at this time was in the second year of the French Revolution, but José Bonifácio and his companions completed their studies in 1791.

The next stop was Freiburg in Saxony, where they studied mining methods. There were not only eminent teachers there, but also silver, copper, zinc, and arsenic mines. The excellent facilities and teachers kept José Bonifácio busy in Freiburg from 1792–1794, when he received a certificate for completing the studies of the mining industry. At Freiburg he realized more than ever how far Coimbra was behind other European universities.

In Freiburg, also, José Bonifácio became well acquainted with Alexander von Humboldt, a brilliant young Prussian scientist who was later to win fame for his scientific expedition to Latin America. Although José Bonifácio made many trips to other parts of Europe in the years following 1794, Freiburg remained his headquarters. He and his companions studied the mining methods of Bohemia (modern Czechoslovakia), Hungary, Prussia, Sweden, Norway, Scotland, and Spain. He returned to Lisbon in September, 1800, after ten years and three months of travel and study. He was now thirty-seven years old, and he had become well known as a scientist.

In 1801 José Bonifácio was authorized to create a course of metallurgy at the University of Coimbra. A short time later he was also named Intendant General of the Mines and Metals of the Kingdom and a member of the Tribunal of Mines. Next he was charged with administering the old coal mines of Buarcos and with restoring the abandoned iron foundries of Figueró dos Vinhos and Avelar. In the same year of 1801 he was named director of the Royal Laboratory of the Mint of Lisbon, with instructions to set up chemical experiments. In the following years other duties were added to this impressive list.

It was obviously impossible for José Bonifácio to be in so many places at once, and his efforts were also hampered by indifference and passive resistance to change. He did not enjoy teaching, and after having studied in the best European universities, he found the instruction at Coimbra antiquated and ineffective. Most of the reforms Pombal had tried to introduce were effectively resisted. José Bonifácio gathered together an excellent collection of minerals for study, but few students showed any interest in them.

Weary of the struggle against indifference, bad faith, and ignorance, José Bonifácio rented a farm near Coimbra and turned to the cultivation of wheat, rice, vegetables, and flowers. He intended to become proficient as an agriculturist, and to return to Brazil.

The Baron von Eschwege visited José Bonifácio in his rustic surroundings, and had much to say about the Intendent General of Mines and Metals in his reminiscences of his trip. When showing the baron some worthwhile achievement, José Bonifácio invariably explained that he was responsible. Where censure was indicated, he called the result the work of his assistant, "a burro and an imbecile."

When French troops invaded Portugal late in 1807, José Bonifácio quickly joined the resistance. On various occasions he was publicly praised for his patriotism, knowledge, and valor. The royal family and much of the Portuguese nobility had fled to Brazil when the French approached Lisbon. The king remained in Brazil until 1821.

While José Bonifácio remained in Portugal, Brazil was being changed from a sleepy, tropical colony to a Portuguese kingdom. Many Brazilians came to regard their land as a unique nation. As long as the royal family resided in Rio de Janeiro, Brazil was the center of the Portuguese empire. Once Dom João returned to Lisbon, however, Brazil might become a mere colony once more.

In 1819, when he was fifty-six years old, José Bonifácio returned at last to Brazil. He had spent thirty-six years in Portugal. The first Brazilian problems he sought to solve were abolition of the slave trade and of slavery itself. Like Father Vieira earlier, he hoped to see the Indians brought into the main currents of Brazilian life. He was not appointed to the king's cabinet, however, for Dom João appointed only Portuguese.

In August of 1820 a rebellion broke out in Portugal. The rebels demanded a constitutional monarchy. Similar demands were soon raised in Brazil. In 1821 Dom João reluctantly returned to Portugal. Before leaving his son, Dom Pedro, as Regent of Brazil, Dom João gave him some fatherly advice. If an independence movement developed in Brazil, Dom Pedro should take the lead in it.

The Portuguese soon demanded that Brazil return to her

former subordinate position as a colony. Brazilians refused to accept any position other than that of kingdom, co-equal with Portugal. The Portuguese Cortes insisted that Dom Pedro return to Portugal. He refused. The Brazilians had now taken the first step toward independence. On January 16, 1822, Dom Pedro named José Bonifácio Minister of the Kingdom and of Foreign Relations. He was the first Brazilian to be elevated to the rank of minister.

Dom Pedro was a youth of twenty-three years, while José Bonifácio was nearly sixty. Dom Pedro's education was poor and unsystematic, while José Bonifácio was one of the great scientists of the day. Dom Pedro was romantic as well as ambitious. He greatly admired Napoleon; his wife, Leopoldina of Austria, was the sister of Napoleon's Empress Maria Luisa. Dom Pedro had a romantic belief in constitutional monarchy, though his upbringing was that of an absolute monarch. José Bonifácio believed in a realistic approach to government, and he did not feel that Brazilians were ready for self-government.

Despite all these contrasting views and the differences in their ages, the two men became warm friends. Each was certain his own opinions were correct, and their disagreements and reconciliations were dramatic.

José Bonifácio believed in democratic and responsible government, but he was convinced that there were certain steps that had to be taken to achieve it. First it was necessary to abolish slavery and to incorporate the Indians into Brazilian life. The huge landed estates should be broken up, and immigration should be encouraged. Without these basic steps he feared that a sudden plunge into democratic government would result in the country falling apart. Keeping Brazil united, he believed, was the main duty of the government at that time. Unfortunately, he was unable to work in harmony with those about him.

There had been, in the past, several republican uprisings in Brazil. One of these, the Mineiro Conspiracy of 1789, had been in the populous state of Minas Gerais. Before Brazil broke completely away from Portugal, it was necessary to know whether the monarchy would be continued or a republic established. José

Bonifácio, fearing the tumult that was occurring in Argentina and other former Spanish colonies, was convinced that Brazil could avoid chaos only by continuing the monarchy. He urged Dom Pedro to visit Minas Gerais, to learn the attitude of the *mineiros.*

The trip to Minas Gerais was a distinct success, for the people of the province expressed wholehearted support of Dom Pedro. The moment for declaring independence was approaching, but the time was not yet ripe.

The Masonic Order, which had been established in Brazil in the 1790's, was active in its support of the idea of independence. José Bonifácio joined the lodge in Rio de Janeiro. The Masons, being one of the few organized groups in Brazil, would play a leading role in the movement for independence. The Rio lodge gave Dom Pedro the title of "Perpetual Protector and Constitutional Defender of Brazil." Some of the leading Masons believed that by bringing Dom Pedro into the secret society they would be able to control him. José Bonifácio was not so easily misled. Dom Pedro, he knew from experience, was not a man who would permit himself to be managed.

A revolt seemed to be brewing in the province of São Paulo. To restore tranquillity there, José Bonifácio believed that Dom Pedro's presence was required. While Dom Pedro was on this journey, insulting dispatches arrived from Lisbon. The Portuguese Cortes annulled Dom Pedro's acts and called him a traitor. After reading the dispatches, José Bonifácio and Dona Leopoldina were convinced that the time had come for a declaration of independence. They sent a messenger racing after Dom Pedro.

On September 7, 1822, the messenger found Dom Pedro near the stream of Ypiranga. After hastily reading the messages, Dom Pedro exclaimed: "The time has come! Independence or death! We are separated from Portugal!" This was the "Grito de Ypiranga," Brazil's declaration of independence.

On October 12th Dom Pedro was named constitutional emperor of Brazil. Forming the new government proved a difficult task, for many men with no experience were convinced that they alone knew how to govern. There was no spirit of compromise visible anywhere.

To José Bonifácio slavery remained the fundamental problem to be resolved. He had already freed the slaves on his family estate, and he had demonstrated that land could be worked successfully with free labor. He asked Caldeira Brant, future marquis of Barbacena, to send families of free immigrants from England.

The constitutional assembly moved slowly, though its debates were heated. José Bonifácio's brothers Antônio Carlos and Martim Francisco were among the most active members. The deputies were divided into groups and factions, and their quarrels delayed the work on the constitution. Dom Pedro grew impatient.

In Portugal, Dom João recovered his former powers and threw out the constitution. Brazilians began worrying about Dom Pedro's absolutist tendencies, especially as he increasingly chose Portuguese rather than Brazilians as his associates and advisers. The Andrada brothers were especially opposed to permitting Portuguese officers to command Brazilian troops.

As time went by and the constitutional assembly got no nearer to finishing its work, Dom Pedro's impatience grew. Finally he ordered the deputies to disband. José Bonifácio and his brothers were arrested, for Dom Pedro had been captivated by his Portuguese advisers. On their advice he sent the Andradas into exile.

The vessel in which the exiles traveled was a captured Portuguese transport that was in no condition for sailing. The enemies of the Andrada brothers apparently hoped ship and passangers would be captured by a Portuguese warship. The captain was Portuguese, and though his orders were to land the exiles at Le Havre, France, he sailed slowly past Lisbon. On January 30, 1824, a storm so damaged the ancient craft that the captain put into the Spanish port of Vigo for repairs. Soon afterward a Portuguese corvette sailed into port and anchored nearby.

José Bonifácio wrote to the Spanish governor general and demanded that he have them transferred to a neutral ship. The governor general ignored the letter. José Bonifácio then wrote to

Prime Minister George Canning of Great Britain. In July the Brazilians were permitted to land and proceed to France. They settled in Talence, a village near Bordeaux.

Martim Francisco and Antônio Carlos were permitted to return to Brazil in April, 1828. In the following March, José Bonifácio was allowed to end his exile. The voyage was saddened by the death of his wife, Narcisa O'Leary. José Bonifácio was now sixty-five years old, poor and weary. He wanted only to rest in the sun at Santos, but his services were still needed by his country.

Dom Pedro's early popularity was completely gone, and opposition to him was rising. After dissolving the constitutional assembly he had given the country a constitution, but he was never able to rule constitutionally. Because Brazilians were likely to oppose some of his views, he had depended almost entirely on Portuguese.

When José Bonifácio called on the emperor, Dom Pedro received him with unconcealed delight. José Bonifácio believed that the troubles could still be surmounted if Dom Pedro chose a cabinet of able Brazilians, but it was too late.

In April, 1831, Dom Pedro abdicated in favor of his young son, Dom Pedro II. Before leaving Brazil, Dom Pedro appointed José Bonifácio as tutor and guardian for the future emperor.

The Chamber of Deputies felt that it, not Dom Pedro, should choose the tutor for the royal children, and José Bonifácio was soon under attack. Padre Diogo Antônio Feijó, Minister of Justice, was determined to appoint another tutor in his place. In December, 1833, José Bonifácio was dismissed. He was never paid for his services as tutor, though his salary was supposed to equal that of cabinet members. The chief charge against him was his opposition to slavery.

The remaining five years of his life were spent in the quiet of his home at Paquete. At last he had the time and solitude for reading and contemplation, and for enjoying the visits of his brothers and their children. He died on April 6, 1838, at the age of seventy-five.

José Bonifácio's great services earned him the title of "Archi-

tect of Brazilian Independence." He had feared the chaos and anarchy that independence had brought to Spanish America, and he
had labored hard to spare Brazil a similar ordeal. His efforts were
not in vain, and though they were forgotten by his contemporaries, later generations remembered him with affection and gratitude.

Cândido Mariano da Silva Rondon
1865–1958

One of the most unusual careers of any man in the Western
Hemisphere during the past century was that of Cândido Rondon. He was born in the frontier state of Mato Grosso, Brazil, and
he attended school in Cuiabá. His father, Silva, died before he
was born. His mother died soon afterward, and he went to live
with his grandfather on a cattle ranch near Cuiabá. Later he went
to live with a relative named Rondon, whose name he added to
his own.

Rondon's grandmother was an Indian woman, and he had other
ancestors who were part Indian. Rondon was, therefore, a mestizo.
But unlike many mestizos or other mixed bloods, he had affection
for all his parent stocks. Too often people of mixed ancestry tried
to hide the fact, and felt ashamed of their Indian or Negro fore-
bears. Rondon became Brazil's greatest friend of the Indian.

In 1879 he attended the Escola Normal, or Normal School,
completing the courses in 1881, when he was sixteen. After that
he joined the Army, and worked his way into the Escola Militar.
There he studied mathematics under Benjamim Constant, the Brazilian Positivist leader who was one of those who helped bring
about the overthrow of the empire in 1889 and the establishment
of the Republic. In 1890 Rondon earned a degree in mathematics
and natural sciences.

After serving briefly as a mathematics instructor, Rondon returned to Mato Grosso and took charge of laying telegraph lines to distant frontier posts. He spent many years in the Brazilian wilds, becoming Brazil's foremost explorer. Brazil was not even mapped, and much of the area was known only by uncivilized Indian tribes. He returned to Rio de Janeiro on various occasions, and in 1892 married Teresa Xavier.

The telegraph lines were of copper wire, and the wild tribes cut the wires to use for ornaments. When Rondon took up his work, the Army had developed the practice of punishing the Indians by killing them on sight. Being partly of Indian blood, but also because of his tremendous love of humanity, Rondon persuaded Army officers to permit him to try kindness instead of force. As former President Theodore Roosevelt said of him later: "In dealing with the wild, naked savages he showed a combination of fearlessness, wariness, good judgment, and resolute patience and kindness. The result was that they ultimately became his firm friends, guarded the telegraph lines, and helped the few soldiers left at the isolated, widely separated little posts."

Before Rondon began his work, the troops were needed to discipline Indians. Once he persuaded the Indians to leave the wires alone, most of the troops were withdrawn, except for a few men needed to make repairs. The Indians saved the maintenance crews much time by reporting when trees had fallen across the lines.

In 1898 Rondon entered the Positivist Church. To him it was the religion of all mankind. The Brazilian Positivists had opposed the monarchy as being "unscientific." They had opposed slavery for the same reason. The author of the Positivist doctrines, the Frenchman Auguste Comte, had many followers throughout Latin America, but they were by no means uniform in their views. Rondon was a devoted friend of the Indians. The Positivists of Mexico in the same period believed in white supremacy.

Because of his Positivist views Rondon did not support the Catholic Church's program of missionary work among the Indians. The Church, of course, was not enthusiastic about civilizing the Indians through the Army rather than through the Church. There was not, however, hostility between them.

On one occasion Rondon discovered the remnants of a small tribe that had been almost completely exterminated by the Army and the settlers. He assembled some volunteers to help him try to win the confidence of these frightened and harried people. There must be no violence or threat of force, he warned them. They agreed to the oath he prescribed—"To die if necessary, but never to kill, even in self-defense."

Rondon had great skill in winning the confidence of the wild tribes, owing perhaps to his appearance, his Indian features, his good humor, and his ability to convince the Indians of the justice and fairness of his every action. All this was done without ever firing a shot, even though many of his companions were killed, and he himself suffered two arrow wounds.

It was not simply a matter of Rondon persuading the Indians to trust him. First he had to convince the Brazilians that this unique and untried approach was the right one, not only because of its humanitarian qualities but also because it could succeed. By convincing them that the Indians could gradually be brought voluntarily into the mainstream of Brazilian life, Rondon revived the long-ignored plan of José Bonifácio de Andrada, who had urged this course as vital to Brazil's future. Rondon consciously followed José Bonifácio's plans, and gave credit where it was due. He honored his predecessor by naming the westernmost of the frontier posts he established "José Bonifácio."

Even after rising to the post of Director of the Commission of Strategic Telegraph Lines, Rondon insisted on continuing his explorations. In 1907 he was in charge of exploring the unknown zone from Mato Grosso to the Amazon River. A large part of his time was spent in collecting specimens and information on the flora, fauna, and natural resources.

During these years of tireless explorations Rondon produced sixty-six publications. He collected more than 8,000 botanical specimens and more than 6,000 zoological specimens. As Artur Neiva said, "No Brazilian scientific expedition contributed so much to the development of natural history among us and none won so much fame abroad."

His ethnological studies—descriptions of living peoples—were also tremendous contributions. Rondon worked also as a geographer. He did not attempt to do all the scientific investigation by himself, but took along various scientists on different expeditions. These men also suffered the hardships characteristic of wilderness explorations.

One of his most arduous expeditions was from May to December, 1909, when he traveled from Tapirapoan to the Madeira River. For the last four months he and his companions were without food except for game. They barely survived the ordeal, and Rondon's expeditions earned a reputation for hardships. Many men were reluctant to serve on them. Those who did received seven times their regular pay. On one occasion Rondon tried to recruit a cook off a little river steamer. "Senhor," said the cook in pretended horror, "I have never done anything to deserve punishment!"

Because of Rondon's quiet, determined, and successful efforts with the Indians, he finally convinced Brazilian officials to support his plans. In September, 1910 President Nilo Peçanha authorized establishment of the Serviço de Proteção aos Índios, or Indian Protective Service, and named Rondon as Director. Those who took service with this new federal agency had to swear the oath Rondon had adopted for himself years earlier—"To die if necessary, but never to kill." This was the official adoption of the plan of José Bonifácio.

In 1913 the Congress of Races in London applauded the program of Brazil and Rondon. Despite the Church's disapproval of Rondon's Positivist faith, he was generally hailed as a great humanitarian, and Brazil was held up as an example to be followed in race relations.

In this same year Rondon and former President Theodore Roosevelt joined in a long expedition to explore the Rio da Dúvida, or River of Doubt, which had never been followed to its source. Several scientists and Roosevelt's son Kermit accompanied them. The two leaders became great friends. In his *Through the Brazilian Wilderness* Roosevelt mentioned *canja,* a thick soup of chicken and rice, and said there was "nothing better of its kind." In his account Rondon also mentioned Roosevelt's enjoyment of this soup, and said Roosevelt's only two words in Portuguese were "mais canja" (more *canja*).

A stream which entered the Rio da Dúvida Rondon named the Rio Kermit. At a formal celebration far in the Brazilian wilderness, Rondon read an official order renaming the Dúvida itself the Rio Roosevelt. This upper section of the Madeira River still bears Roosevelt's name. After the reading Rondon led three cheers for the United States, for Roosevelt, and for Kermit. Roosevelt responded by calling for cheers for Brazil and Rondon.

During the 1920's Rondon served in various military assignments, such as commander of the forces in Paraná and Santa Catarina. He was at his post in 1924 when the São Paulo revolt occurred. In 1927 he was back inspecting the frontiers, in the country he loved.

In 1930 the Vargas revolt changed Brazil from the Old Republic to the New State. Rondon continued to serve in various capacities. In 1934 he was named Delegate of Brazil and President of the Mixed Commission to solve the Leticia dispute between Colombia and Peru. He conducted this difficult task with great tact and obvious humanitarianism, and ultimately brought the contenders to an agreement.

In 1939 Rondon retired from active service, but he still worked with the Indian Protective Service. He was much involved with it during the 1940's, when the Service tackled its most unpromising task—to win the confidence of the Chavantes.

The Chavantes had never been conquered or even approached successfully. They lived on the slopes of the Roncador Mountains, and were huge, powerful warriors. The Rio Xingú was the border of their hunting grounds. In 1650 some frontiersmen had tried to force their way across the river. They suffered such shocking losses that they named the stream the Rio das Mortes (River of Deaths), and this name still appears on maps.

Other parties had tried equally unsuccessfully to fight their way into Chavante country, but none succeeded. A number of daring explorers also ventured across the Rio das Mortes. What happened to them can only be guessed, for none was ever seen again. Most famous of these was the British officer Percy W. Fawcett, who vanished in 1925. In 1934 two missionary priests paddled down the Rio das Mortes in a canoe. Their bodies were found by diamond prospectors on the riverbank.

In the 1940's Brazil was involved in the laying out of emergency airfields across the breadth of the land. Before this time commercial flights were obliged to follow the coastline. This made flights to Rio de Janeiro from the United States a day longer than they would have been if they had been able to go directly across the interior.

One of the parties sent to lay out airfields was the Roncador-Xingú Expedition, named for the mountains and river of Chavante land. Before it reached the Rio das Mortes, efforts had been made to soften the hostility of the dreaded Chavantes.

Small planes flew over the clearings in the Chavante country, and dropped mail sacks filled with gifts for the Chavantes. The pilots then circled to watch. What they saw gave them little cause for encouragement, for the tall, muscular warriors beat on the sacks with huge clubs. Some of the planes flew over the Chavantes. When the pilots landed at their own airstrip, they found arrow holes in the fabric wing coverings.

Metal planes were brought out from Rio, and the softening process continued. On several occasions the pilots became irritated at the Chavante actions. They dived their planes into the clearings, straight at the groups of warriors. Arrows rattled against the metal bodies of the planes. The Chavantes did not flinch, but stood their ground, brandishing their clubs, and throwing them at the planes.

The expedition stopped across the river from the Chavante country and began building the town of Chavantina. In December, 1941, seven men from the Indian Protective Service crossed the river and approached one of the Chavante villages, while twenty others waited in camp. Only one of the seven escaped. The Chavantes then attacked the main camp and killed the others.

There was a tremendous outcry in Rio, and demands that the Army be sent in to teach the Chavantes manners, to take revenge. But Rondon was in charge, and he refused to be pushed into violence against the Indians. He told the reporters that there would be no reprisals. His only immediate act, he told them, was to send in another party to recover the bodies, if possible.

The planes continued dropping gifts, while the expedition worked on Chavantina. The Chavantes, their curiosity growing, watched from the opposite bank of the Rio das Mortes. They began to try to attract the attention of the "white Indians" across the river. The expedition members, under orders from Rondon, ignored them.

The pilots began reporting that the Chavantes no longer smashed the evil spirits out of the mail sacks, but eagerly opened them. The process of winning over the Chavantes was painfully slow, but in the end Rondon's policy was successful. In September, 1946, four hundred warriors came to the Service's camp bearing blunted spears, a sign that they came in peace. Soon after this, they agreed to a treaty allowing the expedition to cross their country without molestation. In Rio, Marshal Rondon summed up the matter. "This," he said, "is a victory of patience, suffering, and love."

In 1943 one of the newly organized territories of the vast interior was named Rondonia. This was the area around Rondonópolis, in Mato Grosso. Rondon had, during his long life, received an incredible number of honors from other nations as well as from his own. On one occasion Theodore Roosevelt had praised him in extravagant terms, comparing him to the Panama Canal. Since Roosevelt regarded the Canal as his major monument, this was the highest praise imaginable.

Rondon's humanitarian work in behalf of the Indians was an extraordinary episode in the history of the Western Hemisphere. It was a combination of sixteenth-century missionary zeal and the humanitarianism of the eighteenth-century Enlightenment. It was also typically Brazilian, and a reflection of the thought of José Bonifácio. Elsewhere, Indianist novelists protested the centuries of mistreatment of the Indians, and in some areas shamed governments into reluctant and halfhearted action to alleviate the suffering of the Indians. These were, however, only semihumanitarian measures in comparison to those of the Indian Protective Service of Brazil. Not one of them adopted as its motto: "To die if necessary, but never to kill." Rondon was the only Indian hunter who loved Indians.

PART III

Federalist and Centralist

José G. Artigas is remembered as the independence hero of Uruguay. This is a role he did not seek, for Artigas was well aware that Uruguay did not possess the resources or population necessary to embark on an independent national career. His goal was a federal republic in the Río de la Plata region, with provinces such as his own retaining the right to manage their own local affairs. He fought endlessly to prevent Buenos Aires from dominating all other cities and provinces, as the people of Buenos Aires were determined to do.

Most of the other provinces of the former viceroyalty of Río de la Plata also embraced federalism, and they made Artigas their spokesman. He organized the "Liga Federal," and waged war with Buenos Aires. He was close to success in his campaign to force Buenos Aires to accept federalism when the Portuguese invaded Uruguay and annexed it to Brazil. Artigas was driven into exile. Argentina and Brazil soon went to war over Uruguay, and when both had exhausted themselves without either achieving a clear-cut victory, they agreed to make Uruguay an independent state. Artigas became, involuntarily, the hero of independence.

Francia was the leader of another province of the same viceroyalty, but he was opposed to any relationship whatsoever with

79

Argentina. Francia established absolute control over Paraguay, and isolated the country completely from all her turbulent neighbors.

José Gervasio Artigas
1764–1850

The tiny Republic of Uruguay, bounded on the north and south by the giants of South America, Argentina and Brazil, is understandably proud of the "George Washington of Uruguay," José Gervasio Artigas.

The career of Artigas was greatly influenced by the land and the times. When Artigas was born, Uruguay was still an isolated segment of the viceroyalty of Peru, which encompassed all the Spanish possessions in South America. The area of Uruguay was far removed from the mainstream of Spanish colonial culture, and few families immigrated into this land of rivers and grass. These few, however, soon established towns along the rivers.

The most important Spanish contribution to life on the Pampa was cattle. First introduced in the sixteenth century, these cattle multiplied until the mid-eighteenth century they were as numerous as the buffalo of North America. The great herds of cattle became the focal point of the economy of the area and produced a new type of Spanish American, the gaucho.

Far removed from the reach of Spanish law, the gaucho lived a wild life. His basic creed was determined by the necessities of self-survival. He was constantly in contact with the Indians of the Pampa, and soon became less of a Spaniard and more a creature of his immediate environment. The change was reflected in intermarriage with the Indians, transformations in language, in dress, and in human values. Essentially the gaucho was a hybrid of the Indian and the Spaniard.

José Gervasio Artigas (1764-1850)
Federalist leader of the Río de la Plata and creator of independent Uruguay.

José Gaspar Rodríguez de Francia '66-1840) El Supremo, the founder and :olute ruler of Paraguay.

Andrés Bello López (1781-1865)
The Venezuelan scholar who became
the cultural scholar of his day.

José Toribio Medina (1852-1930)
The Chilean who became the most pr
ductive scholar of his day.

The life of the gaucho was a lonely one. A small hut where he kept his family was called home. His working equipment consisted of his ever-present horse, his famous bolas, and a skinning knife. With these he faced nature and managed to extract a living by his skill and bravery. His expertness on horseback, his knowledge of the land, and his courage were to serve him well when the time came for him to repel those who would impose change and lessen his freedom. When that day arrived, the gaucho, under the leadership of José Gervasio Artigas, defended his way of life from the Spanish and, later, the ambitious men of Buenos Aires and Brazil.

Artigas was born in Montevideo in 1764. The Artigas family was one of the oldest and most respected in Montevideo. José's grandfather, Juan Antonio Artigas, came from Spain to Buenos Aires, and in 1726 had been one of the founders of the city of Montevideo.

Both his father, Manuel José Artigas, and his grandfather had gained military distinction against the Portuguese and the Indians. The grant of land that was given to Juan Antonio in reward for his services assured the family of freedom from want. When Manuel José Artigas gained title to his father's lands in 1768, the family became wealthy.

Because Montevideo had no royal university, those who obtained an education locally did so at the Convent of San Francisco. This was where Artigas was taught reading and writing, mathematics, Christianity, Latin, and grammar. The priests were mostly Creoles who were liberal in their political philosophies. Among his more notable classmates were Larrañaga, Vedia, Viana, Rondeau, and Otorgués, all men who were to play vital roles in the Río de la Plata's struggle for independence.

During his schooling Artigas was under pressure from his maternal grandfather to become a priest. The military heritage of his father's family was more appealing to the young Creole, however, and he chose the Army.

When Artigas completed his education, his father sent him to manage an *estancia,* or ranch, at Casupá. This was his first encounter with gauchos, and Artigas was captivated by them. He soon left his position on the *estancia* to live as a gaucho.

In 1776 the Viceroyalty of Río de la Plata was created, with its capital at Buenos Aires. The viceroyalty included Argentina, the Banda Oriental, or Eastern Shore (modern Uruguay), Paraguay, and Upper Peru (modern Bolivia). There had always been rivalry between Buenos Aires and the other cities of the region, and this rivalry became more intense after Buenos Aires became the viceregal capital.

Artigas spent several years in the company of the gauchos, gaining an intimate understanding of their social creed and human values. Artigas saw in them a deep sentimentality in spite of the semibarbaric life they led. He also gained an extensive knowledge of the terrain and of gaucho methods of warfare, and these were to prove of great benefit in his later military campaigns. The gauchos came to accept Artigas as their *caudillo,* or chief.

In 1787 the governor in Montevideo issued a call for men to form a corps of *blandengues,* or border guards, as Portuguese raids on the cattle of the Banda Oriental were causing great losses. Artigas left his gaucho companions and enlisted in this new corps. Here he learned the rudiments of military tactics and science. At the end of his stay in the *blandengues* he held the highest rank possible for a Creole, that of major-aide.

In December 1805 Artigas married Rose Villegán. Two children were born, José María and Eulalia. Eulalia died shortly after birth, and Señora Artigas died soon afterward, in 1807.

In May 1810 Buenos Aires disavowed allegiance to Joseph Bonaparte, and the *cabildo,* or town council, of the city proclaimed its right to rule in the name of Ferdinand VII. Montevideo disagreed, and vowed allegiance to the junta of Seville in Spain. With this rupture in the former viceroyalty, conflict broke out in the countryside of the Banda Oriental against the Spanish-controlled junta of Montevideo. The rebels were mainly gauchos under the leadership of Artigas and other chiefs.

The rebels were supported by Buenos Aires, and soon controlled all the countryside except Montevideo. Artigas commanded the provincial cavalry that dominated the area south of the Río Negro. Adjacent to this region was the town of Las Piedras, the center of an agricultural area that supplied the Spanish in Montevideo. Artigas attacked the Spanish forces at Las Piedras on May 18, 1811, and inflicted such a serious defeat that the Spanish were driven back into the confines of Montevideo. He then laid siege to the city.

After Las Piedras, Artigas was well known in the Banda Oriental, and the populace anticipated complete expulsion of the Spanish from the territory. Forces from Buenos Aires under General José de Rondeau joined Artigas in the siege of Montevideo.

In 1811 the Spanish governor of Montevideo appealed to the Portuguese for assistance. Dom João was happy to oblige, as he was interested in controlling the eastern bank of the Plata estuary. In July of 1811, 5,000 Portuguese troops marched into the Banda Oriental. This threat forced Artigas to divide his forces. In the meantime Buenos Aires had been suffering a heavy naval bombardment from the Spanish fleet. This attack, coupled with a patriot defeat in Upper Peru, forced Buenos Aires to begin negotiations for an armistice to protect the city. The armistice with the Spanish was reached in October of 1811, and by its terms all forces other than Spanish were to be evacuated from the Banda Oriental.

Dismayed at the terms of the treaty, and disappointed that his people had not been consulted, Artigas nevertheless began evacuating his forces in obedience to the terms of the treaty. This act marks an important shift in the history of the area and in the elevation of Artigas to the position of absolute leader of the *orientalistas*. It was also the beginning of the rupture between Buenos Aires and the Banda Oriental.

Up to this point Artigas had been purely a military leader, but his leadership now acquired great political and social connotations. This was the result of the famous "Exodo del Pueblo Oriental." The civilian population of the province, leaving homes and personal belongings, followed Artigas, who accepted the responsibility for their welfare. They feared Spanish domination, and they were devoted to the cause of independence. An estimated four-fifths of the population joined the march out of the Banda Oriental, crossing the Río Uruguay, and setting up camp on the west bank of the river. A contemporary described their situation this way: "All the bank of the Uruguay is populated by people from the Banda Oriental. Some live in tents, others under trees, and all exposed to the inclemency of the weather. Yet they manifest such unity and desire that they cause admiration."

By the end of 1812 Buenos Aires resumed the war against the Spanish, and requested Artigas to join in a renewal of the siege of Montevideo. Artigas agreed to the plan only if his forces remained under his control and not that of Buenos Aires. In February of 1813 the siege of Montevideo was resumed, but this time by separate armies, with separate camps and separate standards. One of these was under the command of Rondeau from Buenos Aires; the other was the *orientalista* army under Artigas. The people returned from their self-imposed exile.

The government of Buenos Aires issued a call for a constitutional assembly, and Artigas called together the representatives of the Banda Oriental to elect delegates. The delegates were given strict instructions regarding the seven requirements the constitution had to meet to be acceptable to the Banda Oriental. These were complete political, economic, and social equality with Buenos Aires for all the provinces, and complete autonomy for the provinces over their internal affairs. Artigas did not intend to place his people under the control of Buenos Aires, and he knew that other provincial leaders shared this feeling.

The *orientalista* deputies carried their instructions to the Constitutional Assembly of 1813, only to be refused admittance. The reason for the rejection was the refusal of Buenos Aires to surrender leadership of the Río de la Plata or to accept a position of equality with all the other provinces of the region.

Rejection of the delegates ended any hope of unity among the patriot forces in the Plata, and led to civil war between the federalists and the centralists. It also caused Artigas to abandon the siege of Montevideo in January of 1814.

News of the breach between Artigas and Buenos Aires spread swiftly through the interior. The *porteños* (people of the port of Buenos Aires) branded Artigas a traitor, and put a price on his head. They hoped to isolate Artigas and the federalism he espoused, but his fame spread throughout the other provinces of the interior.

Early in 1814, Entre Ríos and Corrientes joined Artigas against Buenos Aires, and by April, 1815, federalism was accepted by the Banda Oriental, Entre Ríos, Corrientes, Misiones, Santa Fe, and Córdoba. The loose confederation of these provinces represented most of the settled regions outside Buenos Aires.

Buenos Aires attempted to check the spread of the influence of the "traitor" by force, and porteño armies were dispatched to the Banda Oriental to smash Artigas. On February 22, 1814, Artigas defeated a porteño army under General Holmberg at Espinillos. Subsequent victories at Quintana and Concepción in the same month left Artigas in control of the Banda Oriental, with the exception of Montevideo and the area between the Uruguay and Paraná rivers. The Spanish in Montevideo fell to a porteño army in June of 1814, but Artigas approached the city with his army. Buenos Aires opened negotiations, and in July a treaty recognizing provincial rights was agreed upon. The treaty never went into effect, but it did restore Artigas to good standing, for the charge of treason and the price on his head were removed.

In September, Alvear sent a new porteño army into the Banda Oriental, and open war broke out again. In November a small defeat of the porteños checked their march and allowed Artigas time to marshal his forces. In January of 1815 the main bodies of both armies met at Guaybos, and the porteños were soundly defeated. Artigas demanded the withdrawal of porteño forces from the Banda Oriental and the evacuation of Montevideo. In defeat Buenos Aires had little choice, and on February 25, 1815, Montevideo was turned over to Artigas.

In March, Artigas carried the war into the province of Buenos Aires, and began marching on the city. An army under Álvarez Thomás was sent to stop him at Fortezuelas. Here the porteño army mutinied and joined Artigas, and the advance on Buenos

Aires continued. When news of this reached the city, the government resigned. All previous actions against Artigas were denounced by the new government, and the gates of the city were opened to "The Protector of Liberty," the title the frightened porteños bestowed on Artigas. He entered the city and signed a treaty that recognized the autonomy of the Banda Oriental.

With the end of the civil war, Artigas turned his attention to the solidification of his position in the Banda Oriental and to the confederation of provinces adhering to his doctrine of federalism. In both instances he was unsuccessful.

Four years of strife had left the Banda Oriental in chaos. The economy had been ruined, the old political order destroyed; and the wounds of war were unhealed. To alleviate these conditions, Artigas encouraged the re-establishment of agriculture and sought the assistance of local authorities. Smuggling was suppressed and free trade became a reality. Taxes were collected, and a provincial treasury was established. The most important step taken by Artigas as a civil administrator was the formation of a program for the settlement of the remote areas of the province. Perhaps if time had been available, order and good government would have resulted. The Portuguese invasion of 1816 denied him precious time.

Part of the problem was Artigas's involvement with the Liga Federal, the confederation of provinces. This prevented his directing all of his attention to the problems of the Banda Oriental. The basic problem of the Liga Federal was the establishment of some workable form of union among provinces that were completely autonomous. In 1815 the union was workable because Artigas controlled the most powerful military force in the area. But when he was forced to divert his troops to face the Portuguese in 1816, the union quickly began to crumble.

With the connivance of officials in Buenos Aires, and with porteño approval, Portuguese troops crossed into the Banda Oriental in August of 1816. Two main forces made up the invasion. One, of about 6,000 men, marched into the frontier region in the north to prevent a counteroffensive aimed at the Brazilian province of Rio Grande do Sul. The other, also consisting of about 6,000 men, marched directly south along the Atlantic coast. This force was augmented by about 10,000 troops that arrived by sea.

To face these Portuguese armies, Artigas had approximately 8,000 men. About 5,000 of these were deployed to the north to pose a threat to Brazil, and 3,000 were dispatched to stop the advance down the coast.

The first military engagement of the war was at Santa Ana, in southern Brazil, on September 22, 1816. Here the Portuguese checked a counterinvasion led by Artigas himself.

At first Artigas was victorious, but the Portuguese reorganized their forces and attacked the main camp at Corumbe, capturing most of the equipment and supplies. This serious defeat forced Artigas to abandon his offensive in Brazil.

His followers suffered another blow on the coast at India Muerta. Corumbe and India Muerta signaled the beginning of the end, for bravery proved no substitute for numbers, equipment, and discipline. In January, 1817, the Portuguese occupied Montevideo. Artigas laid siege to the city.

At this crucial point Buenos Aires began to attack the provinces of the Liga Federal. Artigas relied on military assistance from these provinces, but the new porteño threat forced them to divert their forces to defend their homes. This action by Buenos Aires contributed as much as the Portuguese invasion to Artigas's ultimate defeat.

In 1819 Artigas attempted a second invasion of Brazil, hoping to force the Portuguese to return to their own country. Under the command of Andresito, Artigas's adopted son, a force was sent into Misiones. Another, under Otorgués, followed through the Banda Oriental. Otorgués was defeated and captured on May 8th, and Andresito met a similar fate on June 24th. These defeats ended the second invasion attempt.

Artigas then crossed the Uruguay into Entre Ríos with 2,000 reinforcements sent by his allies, and attempted a third invasion of Brazil. The same fate awaited him. One wing of his army was defeated by the Portuguese at Ybirapuitan on December 14th. This was followed by successive victories over Artigas that forced him to retreat. The Banda Oriental became the Cisplatine Province of Brazil.

Artigas, after reaching Entre Ríos, attempted to pump new life into the fading Liga Federal. He failed, and in July of 1820 he was forced to take political asylum in Paraguay. There he remained until his death in 1850.

Although his military campaigns ended in failure, Artigas gave force to the idea of federalism in Argentina, an idea that ultimately triumphed in the Constitution of 1852. More importantly, he made the people of the Banda Oriental conscious of their uniqueness. They never forgot that lesson. In 1826 they rose up against the Portuguese, and with British and Argentine aid declared themselves independent of Brazil. The office of president of the new republic was offered to Artigas, but he preferred to leave the rule to younger men. He gave the nation of Uruguay its concept of nationality, and he gave Argentina one of its principal philosophies of government. Such contributions account for Artigas's being honored by the statue in Washington, D.C., identified simply as:

JOSÉ GERVASIO ARTIGAS
FATHER OF URUGUAYAN INDEPENDENCE

José Gaspar Rodríguez de Francia
1766–1840

Dr. Francia, the real founder of modern Paraguay, was born in Asunción on January 6, 1766. His father was a Brazilian who had come to Paraguay to help revive the production of tobacco. His mother was the daughter of a former governor. Francia, who learned to speak and read French, later claimed to be of French descent.

The academy at Asunción provided Francia's early education. He was trained for the priesthood, and at the age of fourteen was sent to the University of Córdoba in northwestern Argentina. Five years later, in 1785, he earned the degrees of Master of Philosophy and Doctor of Sacred Theology.

As a student Francia was remembered as a "bookworm," one given to constant study and deep thought. He had few friends, for he was unsociable by nature. Like other students then and now, he wrote home asking for money. He returned to Asunción in 1786, proud of his doctor's degree, for there was only one other in Paraguay. The title of doctor and his ability to speak French were his chief vanities. Since no one else in Paraguay spoke French at all, Francia was acknowledged to be a gifted linguist. As there was no way of disproving it, Paraguayans generally conceded that he spoke French as flawlessly as a native.

Francia seems not to have considered taking holy orders and entering the priesthood. His hopes for a responsible position in the government were in vain, however, for all such offices were reserved for Spaniards rather than for Creoles. Francia never forgot a slight, and he was deeply offended that a man of his proved talents should be ignored.

The only suitable position he could find was the chair of Latin at the Royal Academy of San Carlos. But because Francia read books that were on the prohibited list without obtaining permission from his superiors, he was soon in trouble. He was particularly fond of Rousseau's works and those of Benjamin Franklin. He made no secret of his admiration for their ideas. As a result the vicar of the academy dismissed him as being too liberal. From this day on, Francia was a sworn enemy of the Church.

There were other examples of his unyielding feelings when once aroused. He quarreled with his father over his refusal to become a priest and over his mother's property, which he felt should pass to him immediately after her death. He withdrew to a house in the country, where he remained isolated with his books. His father gave in, but by this time the damage had been done. Francia would never speak to him thereafter. Years later his

dying father sent relatives to plead with him to come to his bed-
side, for he feared that without a reconciliation with his son his
soul was in danger. Francia coldly rejected the deathbed request.
The qualities of mercy and forgiveness were no part of his
makeup.

After losing the chair of Latin, Francia began practicing law,
although he had no law degree. By choice he represented the
poor and helpless, especially the Guaraní Indians. They came to
regard him as a semideity. A story told of Francia the lawyer was
that a friend asked help in acquiring title to land owned by one of
Francia's enemies. Francia refused to be party to the fraud, and
even threatened to help his enemy. This story may well have
some element of truth in it, but it has the ring of hero legend
reminiscent of a more famous story about chopping down a
cherry tree.

Francia's reputation grew, not only as a protector of the poor
but also as a man of unparalleled learning and wisdom. He not only
possessed the largest library in all of Paraguay; he also knew
what was in those mysterious volumes, all 250 of them. This unrivaled learning made him an awesome opponent—who could tell
what thoughts might be behind those dark eyebrows?

Through the practice of law Francia rose to become attorney
general of Paraguay. In 1809, when the town council of Asunción
elected a deputy to represent the province in the Spanish Cortes,
Francia was the logical choice. He did not, however, make the
journey to Spain.

In 1810, when the movements for independence began in Spanish America, the people of Paraguay did not take immediate action. The Spanish governor, Velasco, called a meeting of the
cabildo, and then assembled the leading citizens, among whom
Francia was prominent. Basing his opinion on Rousseau's idea of
a social contract, Francia argued that Spanish authority reverted
to the people upon the abdication of Ferdinand VII.

The principal threat to Asunción was not Spain but the rival
city of Buenos Aires. Like Artigas and the people of the Banda
Oriental, the Paraguayans refused to submit to domination by

Buenos Aires. Unable to predict the future course of events, the Paraguayans tried to prepare for every eventuality. They swore allegiance to the Spanish Regency, which claimed to be acting in the name of Ferdinand but which was of dubious legality. At the same time they voted to maintain cordial relations with Buenos Aires. After these potential threats were blunted, they got down to the serious business of establishing a junta to separate Paraguay from both Spain and the viceroyalty. They feared rule by Buenos Aires far more than they feared any action by Spain.

The porteños of Buenos Aires, who were engaged in a similar movement away from Spanish rule, quickly perceived that the Paraguayans intended to go their own way rather than remain subservient to Buenos Aires. Early in 1811 a porteño army under General Manuel Belgrano marched toward Asunción, to cow the wayward province with a show of force, and to bring it back into line. The Paraguayans have never been easily pushed, and they met this army with determination. Belgrano was forced to surrender. Since Paraguay had not yet openly broken with Spain, Belgrano's defeat seemed to be a victory for the royal cause.

It was no royalist victory, however, for the Paraguayans were simply meeting their most immediate threat first. Once they felt safe from the porteños, they deposed Spanish Governor Velasco, established a new junta, and declared their independence from Spain. Francia, who had been secretary of the first junta, became the leading member of the second. His rise to supreme power had begun.

The new junta called a national assembly of one thousand representatives. Most of them were from the rural regions, where Francia enjoyed immense popularity. He dominated the assembly from the outset. Some Paraguayans believed that Francia insisted on a large assembly so that it would include some of his most devoted followers. Most of the men would also be anxious to complete their task quickly and return home. This would make them less likely to argue over every point.

The assembly confirmed the second junta, and adjourned. The junta made friendly overtures to Buenos Aires, but remained

watchful against falling under porteño domination. The Paraguayans agreed to a vague treaty binding them to a loose federal
pact with Buenos Aires, but the same treaty acknowledged their
independence.

Francia now took another daring step in his rise toward power,
a step that at first seemed to end his political career. Complaining
that the Army officers dominated the junta, he resigned from it.
For about a year he lived in Asunción, apparently withdrawn
from worldly affairs. To some of his bewildered countrymen he
still exerted a "mysterious influence." He was, in fact, quite busy,
hiding his activity so as not to arouse his rivals before he was
ready.

One reason for Francia's withdrawal was to allow his countrymen to discover that they could not get along without him. Late
in 1812 he allowed himself to be persuaded to rejoin the junta. By
this astute maneuver he had greatly increased his prestige and
made himself seem indispensable. Never again, until his death in
1840, would he relinquish power even temporarily.

In 1813 the treaty with Buenos Aires was renounced, and the
assembly, under Francia's skillful guidance, established the Republic of Paraguay. Borrowing from Roman history, Francia
proposed that two consuls be appointed, to serve alternating
four-month terms in office. The assembly obligingly named Francia and Fulgencio Yegros, a Creole cattleman, as First Consul and
Second Consul. Yegros had some military experience, but he was
totally ignorant of anything outside Paraguay. A story told of him
is that when he heard England was sending a shipload of muni-
tions to Russia for use against Napoleon, he expressed the wish
that the wind would blow the ship all the way up the river to
Asunción.

For one year Francia and Yegros alternated in power. Francia
needed this interlude to prepare for his complete takeover. The
people became accustomed to his rule, and he quietly transferred
Army officers to make sure that all of the strategic commands
were held by men loyal to him. In this same period the government decreed that Spaniards could marry only mestizos or In-

dians, rather than other Spaniards, in order to weaken their position.

In 1814 a new Congress was summoned, and it dissolved the consulate and named Francia dictator for a three-year term. Yegros was simply brushed aside. In 1816, before Francia's term had expired, he called another Congress, and it obligingly named him dictator for life. He was given a salary of 7,000 pesos, but refused it. Money no longer mattered at all to Francia. What he wanted was power over all things and all people.

El Supremo, as Francia was called, ruled Paraguay for the rest of his life. His ideas of government presumably were derived from Franklin and Rousseau, though he ruled as absolute dictator rather than as president of a republic. Though a thorough tyrant, he ruled in the country's interests as he saw them, and he was especially solicitous of the poor. He expressed the hope that in forty years the Spanish American countries would progress to the point that they could enjoy the fruits of liberty and democracy. In this hope he was overly optimistic.

Francia's policies were purposeful and clear. He wanted Paraguay to become a prosperous and peaceful nation, completely independent of all her neighbors. He greatly distrusted Argentina, and when that unhappy land descended into a state of anarchy he sealed Paraguay's borders to avoid infection. He had no ambitions to extend Paraguayan territory. He wanted only to protect his people against the seeds of civil strife that were characteristic of the other new Spanish American republics.

At one time Francia tried to open trade relations with Great Britain. Buenos Aires dominated the mouth of the Río de la Plata, and Francia's effort was in vain. The porteños imposed unequal duties on Paraguayan goods, so that in order to trade the Paraguayans were obliged to pay tribute to Buenos Aires. The purpose of these discriminatory duties was, the porteños admitted, to force Paraguay to reincorporate with the other provinces of the Río de la Plata.

Francia reacted by cutting Paraguay off from most contacts with other nations. Trade and diplomatic relations were opened with Brazil in 1824, but they were broken off abruptly four years later when Brazilian troops crossed Paraguayan territory without permission.

Thus isolated from her neighbors, the little hermit nation remained virtually free of domestic strife during Francia's long rule. Only Brazil and Chile were able to maintain relative domestic peace in this era, while every other Latin American nation suffered from chronic political instability. In 1829 the governor of the Bolivian province of Santa Cruz wrote to Francia requesting the opening of trade relations. Bolivia was a turbulent land, and the request was flatly rejected. It did not take Francia long to make this decision. The envelope containing the governor's letter was endorsed: "Received at eleven A.M., and returned at two P.M."

Even the overtures of Simón Bolívar, most famous of all the South American liberators, were coldly rejected. Until neighboring states became orderly and tranquil, Francia refused to permit any intercourse with them for any reason.

Francia was a man of swarthy skin, black hair, and piercing black eyes. He combed his hair straight back, and it fell over his shoulders. His dress was a black suit with golden buckles at the knees, and golden buckles also adorned his shoes. In addition, he wore a scarlet cape. This was his dress for most of his life.

Although he had quarreled with his father over money, once he had tasted power he wanted nothing else. He lived frugally and simply, and no one ever dared give him a present. He had no friends or confidants because he trusted no one. He demanded absolute honesty on the part of the officials, and checked their books himself. Anyone caught attempting to defraud the state was subjected to severe and humiliating treatment.

Francia's rule was absolute, and he was the law as well as the government. He defended this by quoting Rousseau. "When the motherland was in danger," said Rousseau, "even Sparta let her laws lie dormant."

In 1820 a plot against Francia was discovered, and he suppressed it ruthlessly, to discourage other attempts. About fifty men were executed, including the former Consul Yegros. The suddenness and severity of Francia's reaction were frightening, and thereafter no one dared oppose him in any way. Even foreigners could not leave the land without his express permission. The French scientist Bonpland was near the Paraguayan border on a scientific expedition. Francia's men captured him, and even though most of the courts of Europe demanded his release, Francia refused to allow him to leave. He gave Bonpland complete freedom of movement within Paraguay, and Bonpland came to love the little country so deeply that he lost his desire to leave it.

Paraguay was entirely dependent upon agriculture, and under Francia's close supervision the country became self-sufficient. He encouraged the raising of cotton and the weaving of cloth, to take the place of what was previously imported. The production of *yerba maté,* or Paraguayan tea, and the improvement of cattle raising were other objects of his attention.

In 1827 locusts destroyed the crops, and there was grave danger of famine. Francia ordered a second crop planted. The people were saved from hunger, and at the same time learned that two plantings were possible.

Francia's life was ever simple. He rose early in the old governor's palace where he lived. After breakfast he wandered about the huge building. At this time of day people came to present petitions and appeals. In the beginning men came personally to present their requests, but the number grew so large and Francia became so obsessed with fear of assassination that his secretary screened all petitions. Those not in proper form were rejected.

In the afternoon, after his siesta, Francia rode in the city or countryside with an escort of cavalry. He visited various projects in progress, and inspected them critically. In the evening he read. All his meals were of simple fare. His life was one of complete loneliness and isolation from comfort and companionship. Even his own brothers and sisters, except, perhaps, for one favorite sister, could not claim him as a friend.

Francia's administrative staff was composed of his secretary,

Patiño, his four Army commanders, and the heads of various government departments. Friendless by choice, he grew fanatic as fear of assassination plots obsessed him. This fear of plots led him to establish an elaborate spy system, and he even had spies to check on other spies. His fears grew to fantastic proportions, and he suspected everyone. He had his food tasted before he ate it, and he slept in a different room every night.

Unlike most other dictators the world has known, Francia cared not at all for high-sounding titles or for the adulation of crowds. Cold and aloof, he cared only for power. Other dictators with far less influence or power frequently directed their most sincere efforts toward looting the treasury. The treasury was one department Francia avoided, leaving its care to two men. Each had a key, and the coffers could be opened only by use of both keys.

Shortly before his death Francia destroyed all his papers. These documents contained evidence of his lifetime's achievements, and their loss makes it forever impossible to reconstruct completely the Francia story. Three months after this act, on September 20, 1840, El Supremo died.

Few writers have ever discussed Francia in sympathetic or objective terms. To most he was a blackhearted scoundrel, a power-mad tyrant, a cold, inhuman recluse. They have ignored the fact that a tyrant may occasionally be a true patriot. Francia had no sense of humor, no light, human touch, in short, no redeeming personal features. He did start his small, isolated country on the road to stability and development. Because of the near destruction of Paraguay in the War of the Triple Alliance (1865–1870), and because her subsequent history has featured instability and poverty, we have forgotten that her story might well have been happier. At the time of Francia's death only Chile had achieved equal stability, and only Brazil was to move out of her turbulent era in the next decade. In other countries men had risen to power with intentions similar to those of Francia, but none of them succeeded for long.

PART IV

Creators of Chilean Culture

Andrés Bello and José Toribio Medina both made enormous contributions to Chilean cultural development in the nineteenth century. Bello was a Venezuelan by birth and a Chilean by adoption, while Medina was a native Chilean.

Chile, a frontier province in the colonial era, achieved political stability more quickly than most of the Spanish American nations. Though the Liberals were a majority, their administrations in the 1820's were chaotic. The Conservatives, who represented the large landowners, were determined that the country should have an effective and stable government. This was one of the few countries in Latin America where the landowning "oligarchs" displayed a sense of political responsibility soon after independence. Because of the political stability Chile enjoyed, she progressed much more rapidly than the other Spanish American republics.

Bello adopted Chile as his homeland, for his native Venezuela was in a state of near anarchy much of the time, and there was no opportunity for intellectual development. He wanted Chileans to develop a culture of their own, and he was a patient, inspiring teacher.

Medina, a shy individual who was curious about many things, devoted his entire life to learning. He worked feverishly, and drove himself constantly. The result was an incredible number of

97

excellent books and articles, which added enormously to his country's prestige among scholars in Europe as well as in the Western Hemisphere.

Andrés Bello López
1781–1865

Born in Caracas, Venezuela, Bello was to become one of the great contributors to Chilean cultural progress. He received his early education in Caracas, and was regarded as an excellent student. His mother and father were both devoted to music, and his father won some fame as a composer of religious music.

Bello's various teachers gave him a love of reading and of books. He studied Spanish and French grammar as well as literature. He also learned to read English, and was especially attracted to Shakespeare's works.

When he was sixteen, Bello entered the university, studying law so as to follow his father's profession. Since his family could not pay for his education, he tutored the children of wealthy families. One of his students was Simón Bolívar, who remained a friend for the rest of his life.

In 1799 the famous scientists Alexander von Humboldt and Aimé Bonpland came to Caracas. Bello became well acquainted with them, and he was thus introduced to the new scientific outlook of the Age of Reason.

In 1802 Bello was given an official post by the governor, and his knowledge of foreign languages made him valuable. When a copy of *The Times* of London was brought from the island of Trinidad, Bello translated the story of the abdication of Ferdinand VII. For the first time Venezuelans learned that Spain no longer had a legitimate Spanish ruler. This news was to inspire independence movements in many parts of Spanish America, for it gave the plotters an excuse. As Morelos and Francia and others argued, since there was no legitimate ruler of Spain, sovereignty reverted to the people.

In 1810 the Venezuelans began their struggle for independence. Bello and Bolívar and Luis López Méndez were sent to England on a mission to obtain British assistance. They persuaded Francisco de Miranda to return to Venezuela to lead the movement, but could not convince the British to aid them. Miranda was foremost among the promoters of independence, and he had spent years trying to persuade England and the United States to aid Spanish Americans against Spain.

Bello remained in England for the next eighteen years, serving as diplomatic representative of his country. His life in Venezuela had prepared him for intellectual activities. His stay in England made him a mature scholar. He became well acquainted with such leading British thinkers as James Mill and Jeremy Bentham. He spent hours poring over books and manuscripts in the British Museum, a world-famous haven for scholars.

In order to make his country and his countrymen better known and appreciated in England, Bello joined José Joaquín Olmedo, a noted Ecuadorian poet, in founding two literary reviews. These publications were short-lived, for the market was small and there were few subscribers. Since his country could rarely pay for his services, Bello supported himself by teaching Spanish and translating.

After completing the liberation of northern South America, Bolívar's star waned and the statesman's troubles increased. The Gran Colombia Bolívar had created out of Venezuela, New Granada, and Ecuador was breaking up, and he had little time for writing letters. Because of this, Bello, who served as the diplomatic agent of Gran Colombia in England, felt that his own countrymen had forgotten him. When he was offered the post of consul general of Gran Colombia in Paris, a post he felt was beneath him, he was offended. Sensing an opportunity to attract him to Chile, Mariano Egaña wrote to his government, urging that Bello be offered the office of Undersecretary of Foreign Affairs. The

Chilean government complied, and Bello accepted. Too late, Bolívar wrote begging him to continue serving Gran Colombia.

When he left for Chile, Bello was a mature and confident scholar of forty-seven. His voice was grave but pleasant. His bearing was dignified and aristocratic. He had a sharp nose, oval eyes, a broad forehead, and round beard. He was, withal, an impressive person, quiet and assured.

Bello and his English wife, Isabel Dunn, reached Chile in June of 1829, and Bello was for the rest of his life one of the principal molders of Chilean cultural and intellectual activity. Chile was a newly independent nation after a long and isolated colonial era. Bello arrived at a critical time, and he sensed the unique opportunity for influencing her cultural development. He quietly but firmly grasped this opportunity, and his contributions were outstanding.

Egaña, who had arranged for Bello to move to Chile, was a Liberal in politics. The Liberals soon fell from power, and the Conservatives set up a strong government to end disunity and chaos. Bello, an outsider at first, chose to remain aloof from and above partisan strife. If he had engaged in it, his achievements probably would not have been worth remembering. He has been criticized for his willingness to serve the government regardless of party in power, but the criticism is undeserved. Egaña and some other Liberals perceived the need for stability, and also supported the Conservative regime. It was Egaña, who, with Bello's assistance, wrote the Constitution of 1833. Bello apparently drafted the articles that guaranteed individual rights and that were similar to those popularized during the French Revolution.

Bello, recognizing the need for stability and order, knew that these could be aided by a rich cultural tradition. He was also convinced that Chile must forget her colonial customs and traditions, and fashion new ones that would encourage growth and development rather than stagnation. The colonial heritage made for a static, unchanging society. It was a poor foundation on which to build a modern, dynamic nation.

One of Bello's first interests was in modernizing and codifying

Chilean laws. In 1833 he declared in a newspaper article that the laws must be codified if constitutional guarantees were to have meaning. While proposals for codification were made, discussed, and then ignored, Bello set to work on the project on his own. By 1840 he had completed two volumes. Three years earlier he had been appointed senator, and he now proposed that a legislative commission be appointed to continue the work. He represented the senate on this commission.

The codification project did not please all Chileans, and criticisms were many. Bello answered them in newspaper articles. His tone was always patient, for he sought to instruct and convince, and to have his work accepted. The protests led to the appointment of a committee to investigate and approve the work on codification. He was called upon to do much of the labor, and his first two volumes served as the model. The work was completed in time to be published and put into effect in 1855.

The code consisted of four parts concerning persons, property, inheritance and gifts, and general obligations and contracts. One of the most valuable aspects of the work was its practicality, a necessity for a new nation such as Chile.

Bello was irritated by the fact that Chileans read little and used Spanish badly. He turned his attention to literary criticism, to preparing a Spanish grammar, and to education. He wrote newspaper articles urging improvement of schools, and he warned Chileans not to expect legislation to solve all problems. He was, in fact, involved in education and grammar from the time of his arrival in Chile.

Mariano Egaña, the Minister of Justice and Public Instruction, urged the establishment of the University of Chile. Manuel Montt, who became Minister of Instruction, asked Bello to help draw up a law for the establishment of the university. There was much debate in Congress over the plan, for the Congress insisted on more governmental control over the university than Bello at first proposed. In 1842 the university was authorized, and it began holding classes in the following year.

There was another debate over who should be named rector.

Montt and Egaña insisted on Bello, and they ultimately won. The Church demanded that the rector be a member of the clergy, and other candidates were proposed. But Bello was Chile's leading intellectual, and his right to the post was generally acknowledged. The inauguration as rector was one of the triumphs of his career.

In his inaugural speech Bello presented his thoughts on national cultural development based on education and research. He urged the establishment of a system of primary education for the whole nation, as he had proposed many times before. In addition, he stressed the need for literary and scientific studies at the most advanced levels. The study of economics in the university should concentrate on national economic statistics and problems. Legal studies should be related to the economy so as to produce genuine social improvement and not merely legal theories. He advocated courses and research in medicine, the sciences, language, the arts, and literature. He emphasized the study of poetry.

In reference to modern sciences, Bello said that they should not be regarded as morally or politically dangerous to society. They were, he maintained, quite necessary for cultural development. Many people feared that scientific knowledge would undermine religious faith, and they opposed the sciences for that reason.

With regard to language and literature, Bello favored the study of ancient languages for the purpose of learning the wisdom, eloquence, and beauty of the high civilizations of the past. These provided inspiration in art and literature that could promote cultural progress. They also made it possible to enrich the Spanish language with new concepts and expressions. Chileans, he said, should analyze and weigh European customs before adopting or rejecting them.

The University of Chile, as Bello envisioned it, was part of a search for liberty in the world of spiritual values. It was opposed to the "servile docility that accepts everything without question." It sought to establish a rational way of life for all Chileans.

The new university had five faculties, which corresponded to colleges in our own universities. These were Philosophy and Humanities, Physical and Mathematical Sciences, Medicine, Law and Political Science, and Theology. The faculty of Philosophy and Humanities was given the responsibility of inspecting the teaching in the national academies, especially with regard to language, national literature, history, and statistics of Chile.

Bello had numerous friends in the new university, such as Egaña, who was dean of the Law faculty. José V. Lastarria, one of his students, became dean of the faculty of Philosophy and Humanities. Another of his former students, the poet Salvador Sanfuentes, was secretary of the university.

The newly established school for the training of teachers was under the general supervision of the university. The first rector of this school was Domingo F. Sarmiento, future "schoolmaster president" of his native Argentina. Another expatriate who served the university was the Polish physicist Ignacio Domeyko. This noted scholar, who had come to Chile at Bello's invitation, was to become the second rector of the university, after Bello's death in 1865.

The university began its operation under considerable control by the government. Though he opposed such interference in academic affairs, Bello was not one for engaging in heated controversies. He worked quietly and calmly to remove political control, and during the twenty-two years of his administration great gains were made in this direction.

Though he did not enjoy controversy, Bello did not shrink from it when it was thrust upon him. Young Sarmiento, who perhaps envied the tremendous prestige Bello enjoyed, jousted with him in the pages of the daily press. Their subject was literature and literary criticism, and Bello responded to Sarmiento's not always friendly attacks as much to instruct the readers as to defend himself. He was as calm as Sarmiento was excitable, and together, by their intellectual exchanges, they greatly stimulated young Chileans to literary activity.

Bello engaged in a similar debate with Lastarria over the writing of history. Bello protested against too much philosophizing. The historian, he maintained, should be as objective and accurate as possible, and should include documentary evidence as proof.

"Learn to judge for yourselves," he advised students of history. "Aspire to independence of thought. Drink at the sources—at least in the torrents nearest to them. The very language of the original historians, their ideas, even their prejudices and their fabulous legends are a part of history, and not the least instructive and true. Would you, for instance, know what the discovery and conquest of America was? Read the journal of Columbus, the letters of Pedro de Valdivia, those of Hernán Cortés. Bernal Díaz will tell you much more than Solís or Robertson. Interrogate each civilization through its works. Demand of each historian that he give his warrants."

To Bello, poetry was the highest form of literary expression, and he was regarded in Europe as Chile's greatest poet. As a youth he had written an "Ode to Vaccination" at a time when inoculation for smallpox was first being introduced, and when many people regarded the treatment with suspicion and even superstition. Bello apparently did not regard this particular poetic effort as immortal, for he kept no copy of it and even forgot it entirely. Probably his most distinguished poetical work was a translation into Spanish of Victor Hugo's "Prayer for All." This difficult task he accomplished with such exquisite skill that a Spanish critic declared that no Spaniard could read it and the original French version without finding Bello's translation the better of the two. He left his mark on New World poetry in another way, too. In 1826, while living in England and perhaps homesick for the Caribbean, he published a poem called "The Agriculture of the Torrid Zone." It may not have been an inspiring subject, and certainly it was not a conventional one, but it proved to New World poets that they could find images and ideas in their own homelands and that they did not need to draw on Europe for them. Bello was ever an Americanist, and he wanted Spanish Americans to create their own cultural forms and foundations and to cease imitating European models.

While working in the British Museum, Bello had gathered copious notes on the different versions of the *Poema del Cid*. For forty years he worked over these notes and texts of the famous epic poem of medieval Spain. This impressive study, which in Spain was called "the major miracle of Spanish philosophy," was not published until 1881, sixteen years after his death.

It was not his poetry, however, that gave Bello his most lasting fame as a writer. In 1847 his *Grammar of the Spanish Language* was published. In his introduction he modestly remarked: "I do not pretend to write for the Castilians. My lessons are directed to my brothers, the people of Hispanic America. I judge it important to conserve the language of our fathers in its purest form. . . . But it is not a superstitious purity that I recommend."

His grammar has been said to have emancipated Spanish from bondage to Latin grammatical forms and rules. It brought about general acceptance of the idea that languages change according to certain identifiable principles related to the characteristics of particular languages. He asserted that Spanish Americans had the right to contribute to the development and enrichment of their language, but opposed the fragmenting of Spanish into different and corrupt dialects. He suggested, as a standard to determine what was proper usage, the way words or expressions were employed by contemporary writers who were known both for learning and for good taste. This criterion of good usage, novel in his day, is widely employed today.

Bello's grammar was used by generation after generation of Chilean students, and it ran through many editions. A new edition came out as late as 1941, and there may have been others since. Though Bello did not pretend to write for Spaniards, the Royal Academy quickly recognized his book, and many Spaniards admired it.

The contributions of this Chilean-by-adoption make an impressive list. His poetry, his beneficial and lasting impact on the Spanish language, and his role in the literary flowering of Chile represent one aspect of his influence. His *Principles of International Law* (1833) and his *Civil Code of Chile* (1855) were influential in Chile's legal and political development. The legal code was, in fact, first in both time and quality on the continent, and it served as the model for many other countries.

The University of Chile is another monument to his memory, and it represents his direct personal influence over individuals and groups. He helped mold the intellectual outlook of two generations of Chileans. He alone could say that the foremost intellectual and political leaders were his students. Few men in any age have done as much for an adopted country.

José Toribio Medina
1852–1930

Among the great historian-scholars Chile has produced, José Toribio Medina holds a special place, owing to the number and variety of his works. He was born in Santiago de Chile, on October 21, 1852. His father was a young lawyer trying to find a professional place for himself. Medina lived with his grandfather on a farm until 1858, when he rejoined his parents at Talca, where his father was a judge. Medina studied at the local academy until his father became a judge in Valparaiso, Chile's main port.

In 1860, Medina attended the Colegio Inglés, or English Academy, of Valparaiso. Two years later his father became paralyzed, and the family was forced to subsist on his pension. Medina continued his schooling in Santiago, where the family moved after his father's illness. In 1865, he entered the Instituto Nacional, which was run by Diego Barros Arana, one of Chile's most famous historians of all time.

The Instituto Nacional, under the inspired direction of Barros Arana, had become the foremost academy in Chile, and it made a deep impact on young Medina. He acquired there the scientific approach to knowledge, the searching, questioning attitude that accepted as truth only what could be proved. In 1869, when he graduated, Medina won the prize in both Latin and natural history.

To please his father, he began the study of law at the University of Chile, though he would have preferred to continue with science. Though he never abandoned his interest in insect life, he heeded his father's warning that law and politics, not bugs, could provide him with a comfortable living.

Because of his lack of funds, Medina worked his way through the five-year law course in three years. In March of 1873 he was licensed to practice law, and was offered several opportunities to enter politics. The politician's life did not attract him; he much preferred his studies of the lives of insects. No doubt his father, who wanted to see him in politics, wondered what he had done to deserve such an odd and ungrateful son. His study of insects led to the discovery of one then unknown, which was named in his honor.

In his field trips in search of specimens and fossils, Medina developed a strong interest in the Indians of Chile. At the same time his interests widened to embrace literature and folklore. He began reading everything written during the Conquest and colonial era. His earliest writings were in literary criticism and on folklore. In 1874, he published a translation of Longfellow's *Evangeline.*

In that same year his father persuaded the minister of foreign affairs to appoint Medina to the Chilean legation in Lima. Medina accepted the post, and in Lima soon became acquainted with the leading writers, one of whom was Ricardo Palma, Peru's famed folklorist. He also became well acquainted with the famous National Library, which had one of the greatest collections of books and manuscripts in South America. In 1875, Medina edited and published a seventeenth-century account of Chile, and his career as a historian was launched.

In the next year Medina wrote four articles on Chilean colonial history. He was now completely dedicated to research on Chilean history, but his interests never stopped expanding.

In 1876, Medina was invited to accompany an Englishman and

his Chilean wife to the United States to attend the Centennial Exposition in Philadelphia. He spent three months traveling in the East and in the Midwest. Then he left for England, where he did research on Chilean literature at the British Museum, as Andrés Bello had done before him. While there he became acquainted with two Spanish scholars. One of these men, Gaspar del Río, was working on a history of the Inquisition in the Netherlands. Medina later made similar studies of the Inquisition in Spanish America.

From England, Medina went to France and Spain, visiting libraries and archives in his search for colonial works concerning Chile. Before returning to Chile, he made a tour of libraries in Italy, Austria, Germany, Belgium, and Holland. In 1877, he returned to Santiago and resumed his practice of law.

In 1878, Medina completed his three-volume history of the colonial literature of Chile. All three volumes won prizes offered by the University of Chile. Because the university could not afford the cost of publishing this important work, Medina used the prize money to bring out the volumes at his own expense. Though he lost money in the venture, Medina had taken his first step in literary history. He had also learned the value of bibliographical research. He was to devote much of his life to both of these activities.

He had also become interested in the native peoples of Chile, especially the Araucanian Indians. In 1879, he went south to the Araucanian country beyond the Bío-bío River. After some 350 years the Araucanians remained unconquered, though their days of independence were nearly over. In 1882, Medina published *The Aborigines of Chile*. No similar anthropological study had been made in Chile, and it was the forerunner of, and model for, many studies of the natives.

The anthropological expedition was interrupted in 1879 by the War of the Pacific, in which Chile defeated Bolivia and Peru. Medina, on hearing of the outbreak of war, hurried to Santiago to volunteer for Army service. He was employed as a civilian in Iquique, where he devised a new and more efficient system for making cartridges. In 1880, he was named judge advocate of the Reserve Army, and a year later was made judge of the province of Tarapacá, which had been wrested from Peru.

Though busy with his official duties, he continued his research and writing. His range of interests was still widening. In these years geography and native languages were added to the list, and he was also co-author of a biography of the naval hero Captain Arturo Prat, who was killed in action during the first year of the war.

In 1883, Medina received an assignment that pleased him immensely. The minister of the interior, José Manuel Balmaceda, asked him to prepare an index to the documents concerning the captaincy-general of Chile. He threw himself into this labor with such zeal that in five months he had made a thorough inspection of more than 18,000 documents and had written a description of them. The volume, published in 1884, contained nearly a thousand pages. As there were not many purchasers for this huge work, the government later sold the remaining copies for scrap paper.

Another opportunity for travel and research came in 1884, when Admiral Patricio Lynch was named Ambassador to Spain. He asked that Medina be made secretary of the Chilean legation in Madrid. Before leaving Santiago, Medina obtained 2,000 pesos from the University of Chile to pay for having documents copied. With this modest sum, and through his own voluntary services, he obtained copies of nearly 16,000 pages of documents. In the famous Archivo General de Indias in Seville, Medina found 700 bundles of documents on Chile. These dated from the Conquest to the beginnings of the movement for independence.

One of the collections that attracted his special attention was that housed in the ancient castle of Simancas. Here he found the archives of the Inquisition. Working in the damp and gloomy dungeon, Medina copied the documents that he later used in his studies of the Inquisition in the Spanish colonies.

Elsewhere he made other important discoveries, such as the

memorial of Fray Luis de Valdivia, which he found in the British Museum. In Toledo he came upon another significant manuscript. It was an account of the civil wars of Peru in the 1540's. He had these and others copied, but he also began purchasing rare books and manuscripts for his own library.

While Medina's interests grew, so did the circle of his friends, especially among the scholars and writers of Spain. The eminent Marcelino Menéndez y Pelayo became a close friend. He nominated Medina as corresponding member of the Royal Academy of Language, and Medina was the first Spanish American to receive this honor. Similar honors came from Madrid's Society of Writers and Artists and from the Royal Academy of History.

The fruitful sojourn in Spain, which seems not to have been hampered by heavy official duties, ended late in 1886. In December of that year he married Mercedes Ibáñez y Rondizzoni, who shared his cultural interests. She became virtually his editorial assistant as well as affectionate companion, and helped in the research, editing, proofreading, and other chores of publication. During the first four years of their marriage, Medina published thirty-one books and three articles. One of the books was the *History of the Inquisition of Lima* (*1569–1820*).

Medina was a man short of stature but physically powerful. He had small blue eyes, and he wore glasses. His manner was nervous. He spoke and moved quickly, and he seemed always to be giving orders. Sometimes he made copyists in the archives so nervous he was unable to read their handwriting. Before his marriage he was considered a rather grumpy recluse. Doña Mercedes changed all that, for she knew he should be on friendly terms with the scholars of Europe as well as of Latin America. On one occasion he admitted, "Whenever I do not follow Mercedes' advice, I am wrong." On many occasions when his nervous manner would have caused doors to be closed rather than opened to him, she gently and amiably soothed ruffled feelings. Without her aid and constant encouragement, Medina's enormous achievements would not have been so great as they were.

In 1888, Medina bought a printing press, and began printing

his own books. The first product of his press was the *Bibliotheca Americana,* a descriptive list of nearly three thousand volumes from his own library. He printed only enough copies to give to his friends and to libraries.

The study of the Inquisition was extended into a series. Each volume was supplemented by a collection of documents, to provide readers with official information on the Holy Tribunal.

In 1890, he brought out his *Bibliography of Printing in Santiago de Chile from Its Origins to February of 1817.* This began a new and important series on printing that eventually comprised forty-six volumes.

In 1891, when President José Manuel Balmaceda was overthrown, crowds went about the streets destroying the property of those who had supported Balmaceda. Medina's home was in danger, but no damage was done to it. When he was invited to Buenos Aires to write a history of the press in the Viceroyalty of Río de la Plata, he was happy to accept. He had already compiled a checklist of books published under the viceroyalty. He sold his press and crossed the Andes on horseback. In five months he had produced a work that a British critic declared merited "a foremost place among bibliographical mammoths."

From Buenos Aires, Medina and his wife sailed for Spain to attend the Fourth Centennial of the Discovery of America, which was held in Madrid. He spent most of his time continuing his research, and while in Spain he published six works, bibliographies and colonial manuscripts, which he edited.

In 1895, after three and a half years of happy activity, Medina returned to Chile. By 1902, he had published seventy-three more books and pamphlets, as well as some articles. He also edited forty volumes of historical documents, most of which were printed in his shop, for he bought another press.

Medina's interest in printing in the Spanish colonies now extended to the Philippine Islands. He published three titles on this subject, and in 1899 brought out a history of the Inquisition in the Philippines.

In 1897, Medina was named to the new Chair of American and

Chilean Documentary History at the University of Chile. He held the post only until 1899, for few students were interested. Though he accepted the position of secretary to the faculty, he devoted all possible time to his research and writing.

Late in 1902, Medina and his wife traveled to Peru, Colombia, Guatemala, and Mexico to collect materials for his series on the colonial press. The Chilean Ministry of Public Instruction, in order to help him to extend his travels in Europe, hired him to study the administration of libraries and archives. He visited France, Switzerland, Italy, and Spain. In Rome he was permitted to use the Vatican Library.

When he returned to Chile in 1904, Medina had collected more than 10,000 books for his library, and over 8,000 pages of notes and copies of documents. He was ready to settle down to more writing. In the next eight years he wrote or edited fifty-nine books and pamphlets and more than a dozen articles. Most of these he also printed on his own press. In 1907, he began printing his eight-volume history of printing in Mexico for the years 1539 to 1821. He completed this enormous task in 1912. In the same period he brought out a history of printing in Guatemala, from 1600 to 1821, a volume of 800 pages. Unfortunately for modern historians, these, like most of his books, were printed in editions of only 250 copies.

By his prodigious efforts and excellent scholarship, Medina had made his name famous among scholars the world over. He had received many honors from foreign academies and governments. Though his accomplishments were almost unbelievable, he still had much to do.

In 1912, the Ministry of Public Instruction again commissioned him to study European archives. The real purpose of the grant was to enable him to complete his search for materials for his critical study of the sixteenth-century epic poem *La Araucana*. He had already published the text of the poem, but wished to follow it with volumes that would include documents, a biography of Alonzo de Ercilla y Zúñiga, author of *La Araucana,* a critical study of different versions of the poem, and the lives of Ercilla's soldier-companions. The series was his greatest achievement in literary history.

On his return to Chile, Medina entered another six-year period of writing and printing. By 1919, thirty-five books and pamphlets and twenty-four articles had been added to his impressive list. In 1919, he sold his printing press and gave up printing his books, but he continued his research and writing at his customary feverish pace. During the last ten years of his life, he published thirty-four books and pamphlets and a larger number of articles.

In 1923, the University of Chile held a great celebration in honor of his fiftieth anniversary as an author. Other universities also held celebrations honoring him, and the University of Mexico conferred on him an honorary doctor's degree.

Moved by these expressions of respect and appreciation, in 1925 Medina presented his enormous and valuable collection to the National Library of Chile. This collection was placed in a specially built room, with mural paintings of various phases of Medina's active career. His library, called the Biblioteca Americana José Toribio Medina, contained over 60,000 printed works, a large number of original manuscripts, and more than 8,500 copies. It was one of the outstanding collections on Spanish colonial history anywhere.

In 1928, Medina attended the Congress of Americanists in New York, then sailed to Spain for the last time. As before, he visited archives and copied documents. Back in Santiago, he continued his work. In the spring of 1930 his health began to fail, and he died on December 11th. At the time of his death he had two manuscripts ready for the printer, and twelve others in various stages of preparation. His total work during his life was nearly 350 volumes in which he had some part, as author, editor, or translator. It is not likely that his record will ever be matched.

PART V

Two Indian Presidents of Mexico

Benito Juárez and Porfirio Díaz were the ablest presidents of nineteenth-century Mexico. Until the death of Juárez they were both associates and rivals. Both were members of the Liberal party, and both fought steadfastly against the French invaders and their puppet emperor, Maximilian. Both were of Indian ancestry, and both knew their countrymen well and how to govern them.

Their aims, however, were quite different. Juárez believed in the ideals of Morelos, and wanted to see Mexico develop into a social and political democracy at the same time the country's economy was improved. Díaz cared little for the political and social objectives of Juárez, but he concentrated on economic development. Both men were sure that they knew better than anyone else what Mexico needed, and both were determined not to relinquish the presidency. The results of their administrations were vastly different. As a result of the leadership of Juárez against the French, Mexico became a nation, but he died before his main goals could be attained. The long rule of Porfirio Díaz produced dramatic changes in the Mexican economy, but it culminated in the Revolution of 1910, when the ideals of Morelos and Juárez were revived.

Before the time of Juárez, Mexico had only one president who served out his entire term of office. Mexico became an independent nation under especially unfortunate circumstances. Her first attempt at independence was the Hidalgo-Morelos revolt, which was an attempt at genuine social revolution. This attempt failed, though many of its ideals persisted. In 1820 there was a liberal revolt in Spain that forced Ferdinand VII to restore the Constitution of 1812. This restoration of the liberal Spanish constitution produced a profound reaction among Mexican conservatives.

In 1820 Mexico was completely controlled by the most privileged and conservative elements, the Church and the Army. The former had amassed great wealth, and it owned an estimated one-half of Mexican property. It paid no taxes, yet the population was obliged by law to pay the tithe or tenth of its income to the Church. Priests also enjoyed the right of being tried in their own courts. The Army was loyal to whoever paid it, and the Church often could outbid the government for Army support. The Army served the Church by crushing movements organized to curtail the Church's privileges and to deprive it of its wealth and political power.

Most of the years from independence to 1855 may properly be called the Era of Santa Anna, for Antonio López de Santa Anna was in and out of office a dozen times during this period. Occasionally he supported liberal movements until the opposition became intense. On such occasions he allowed his vice president to take charge of the government, while he retired to his plantation, Manga de Clavo (Clove Spice), near Veracruz. When the time was ripe he would return as a hero, and help crush his former followers.

Mexico thus had more disadvantages to overcome than most other Spanish American nations after independence. Totally lacking at every level was a sense of political or social responsibility. This irresponsibility on the part of the wealthy and educated class made it possible for adventurers such as Santa Anna to use the government for purely selfish purposes. Though Mexico began her independent existence under unfavorable circumstances, by mid-century conditions were much worse than at the time of independence. Only a tremendous effort could save her from complete ruin, and it would require further efforts to achieve stability and relative prosperity. Juárez supplied the leadership for the first phase. Díaz took charge of the second effort.

Benito Juárez
1806–1872

One of the most remarkable statesmen of Mexico was Benito Juárez, a full-blooded Zapotec Indian from the state of Oaxaca. He was born in an isolated Indian village on March 21, 1806. His parents died before he was three years old. An uncle raised him and taught him to read Spanish.

This experience awakened a burning desire for learning. In 1818 he went to Oaxaca, where he worked for a bookbinder who agreed to help with his education. In 1821 he entered the seminary to study for the priesthood, though his motive was education rather than a desire to become a priest. He extended his studies as long as possible. In 1827 the Liberals created a civil college in Oaxaca. The Church bitterly attacked this school, over which it had no control. Juárez entered the college in 1828, and concentrated on the study of law. In 1831 he began to practice law, and entered politics as an elected member of the city council. A few years later he was elected to the state assembly.

Mexico in this period was in a state of confusion and instability. The Liberals were trying to introduce reforms to limit the political power of the Church. Juárez had an unfortunate experience in trying to defend some poor villagers against a greedy priest. While a Liberal president was in office, the court attempted to conduct a trial of the priest. The Conservatives overthrew the government, and the situation was reversed. Juárez and his clients were imprisoned at the request of the priest. This experience convinced Juárez that the political power of the Church must be broken, and made him a dedicated reformer.

When he was released, Juárez returned to his law practice, and in 1841 became a judge. In 1844 he married Margarita Mazza, of Italian descent, and from one of the leading families of Oaxaca. His wife described him simply but accurately: "He is very homely, but very good," she said. Juárez had come a long way since leaving his native village.

In 1846, with the coming of the war with the United States, the Liberals returned to power. Juárez was elected to the national Congress, and made his first trip to Mexico City. Late in 1847 he returned to Oaxaca, where he became provisional governor. When Santa Anna, fleeing from his defeat by the American army and pursued by a party of Texas Rangers, sought asylum in Oaxaca, Juárez refused. Santa Anna, he knew, was an unprincipled adventurer. Santa Anna never forgave him.

When his term as provisional governor ended in 1848, Juárez was re-elected. He proved to be an exceptional and honest administrator. Knowing well the value of education, he pushed its extension to the rural areas. He also insisted on education for girls. He was aware, however, that poverty was the biggest problem and that education alone was no cure-all. "The man who lacks the wherewithal to feed his family considers the education of his children a very remote benefit or an obstacle to providing their daily bread," he wrote. The building of roads was one way he tried to combat poverty, to make commerce easier.

As governor, Juárez won the cooperation of the Church, for which he was later criticized by his own Liberal party. Had he devoted his energies to battling the Church, however, he would have accomplished little. The Church problem was national, and could not be settled locally. The country was gradually becoming aware that the Church should be forced to abandon its political activities and to dedicate itself solely to its spiritual role.

In 1853 Santa Anna returned to power once more, for the last time. Juárez was arrested, confined in a cell below sea level in the fortress of San Juan de Ulúa at Veracruz, then placed on board an English ship. Passengers paid for his passage to Havana, and from there he sailed to New Orleans, where he found a group of Liberal exiles like himself. He was now forty-seven years old, and he did not appear to be a man who could lead his country through its most trying times.

In New Orleans, Juárez met Melchor Ocampo, a man of wealth and social standing, and a former governor of Michoacán. Ocampo was one of the Liberals' leading thinkers, and his influence on Juárez was great. The little group of refugees plotted the downfall of Santa Anna. Their hopes rose when they learned that Juan Álvarez, an Indian general and an old revolutionary, had started a rebellion in the state of Guerrero. They sent Ignacio Comonfort as their emissary to Álvarez. Álvarez welcomed their support.

In June, 1855, Juárez sailed to join Álvarez in Acapulco. The general was absent when he arrived, and his son did not catch Juárez' name. "Knowing that men are fighting for freedom here, I came to see what way I could be useful," Juárez told him, and was accepted as a mere recruit. He began by serving as secretary to Álvarez.

A few days later a letter addressed to Lic. Don Benito Juárez came, and Álvarez asked him if he were a lawyer. "You mean that you are the same man who was governor of Oaxaca?" he exclaimed. "Why didn't you tell me?"

"Why should I? What does it matter?" Juárez replied.

Juárez immediately became political adviser to Álvarez, who was a fighter but no statesman. Santa Anna fled the country, and the Liberal army marched to the capital. Álvarez became interim president, a role that worried him, and for which he was ill prepared. Comonfort headed the cabinet; Juárez was named Minister of Justice and Public Education. Comonfort, though a Liberal, believed in compromise. Juárez forced his hand by pushing through the Ley Juárez, a law that abolished the special courts of the clergy and placed priests under the jurisdiction of the civil courts.

Revolt was immediate. The Church was determined to retain its privileges, and the Army was worried that its privileges might also be lost. Governor Manuel Doblado of Guanajuato raised the

cry of "Religion and Privileges." On the same day, Alvarez resigned as president in favor of Comonfort. Juárez also resigned
from the cabinet, and was appointed governor of Oaxaca.

In June, 1856, the Ley Lerdo was passed. It forced the Church
to sell its properties. Both of these severe reforms were incorporated in the Liberal Constitution of 1857. When the constitution
was promulgated, the archbishop threatened with excommunica-
tion anyone who swore allegiance to it. Comonfort was elected
President; Juárez was chosen president of the Supreme Court,
which made him next in line for the presidency, as the constitution did not provide for a vice president. Comonfort also named
him Minister of the Interior.

Juárez was imprisoned briefly as one conspiracy followed another. In January, 1858, he was released, and quietly left the capital on foot. Comonfort was ousted, and the Conservatives took
over. Up to this time all Liberal works had been, as the Liberal
poet Guillermo Prieto said, merely prefaces. Juárez was determined that this time the work would be completed, not merely
initiated. He had the conviction, courage, and steadfastness
needed for the long and trying ordeal. In addition, in his own
quiet way, he had the power to attract devoted and equally determined supporters.

As legal successor to the deposed Comonfort, Juárez established his government in Guadalajara. In the Battle of Salamanca,
however, the Constitutional forces were routed. Juárez received
the bad news coolly. "Guillermo," he said to Prieto, "our cock has
lost a plume."

The next day a company of troops were persuaded by the local
priests to mutiny and seize Juárez and his ministers. Then, learning that loyal troops were coming, the mutineers declared a truce
and called for a conference. A captain who knew nothing of the
truce tried to rescue the government, but failed. Angered, the
rebel troops entered the room where the prisoners were held and
prepared to kill them. Juárez, head erect, faced them, but Prieto
leaped in front of him, and began haranguing the soldiers. "You
want blood?" he asked. "Take mine." The soldiers lowered their

guns, and retreated, swearing they would not kill the prisoners.

The truce was resumed, and the mutineers marched out of the city. Prieto remembered this incident vividly twenty years later. Juárez, who was less of a poet, merely recorded in his diary: "On the 13th the Palace Guard rose, and I was made prisoner. . . . On the 15th I recovered my liberty."

The incident reacted in favor of Juárez and his ministers, whose courage had been put to severe test. A few days later, Juárez issued a proclamation to play down the defeat at Salamanca. "Whether or not we lose battles," he wrote, "whether we perish by the light of combat or in the darkness of crime, the sacred cause we defend is invincible. . . ." His quiet courage, displayed without the melodramatics of a Santa Anna, was infectious. Men believed him when he said: "Democracy is the destiny of humanity in the future; freedom is its indestructible weapon, and possible perfection the goal toward which we are going. . . . The idea is above the domain of the cannon."

Juárez proved right. Men may be shot, but not ideas. By making himself the symbol of a cause rather than a personal leader of devoted followers, he was ensuring ultimate victory even though he might be killed before it was achieved. The ideas he stood for would live on in the minds of men.

Juárez and his ministers left for Colima with only a small escort. The outnumbered Constitutionalist forces lost Guadalajara soon afterward. Plans for conduct of the war were altered. General Santos Degollado was placed in complete charge of military operations, while Juárez and the civil government made Veracruz their residence.

Veracruz was traditionally Liberal, it was easily defended, and it provided customs duties. To reach it, however, they had to sail from Manzanillo to Panama, cross the Isthmus, and sail to Cuba and New Orleans.

Juárez and his entourage stayed at a boardinghouse in Veracruz. The woman who ran it did not see him till the next morning, when he appeared and called for water. Thinking he was a servant of the president, she told him to fetch it himself, which he meekly did, to the amusement of his friends. At dinner the woman saw him seated at the head of the table, and was terrified at her error. She fled from the room amid general laughter.

Most of the professional soldiers and ablest officers adhered to the Conservative cause, and the Liberals had to rely largely on civilians-turned-soldiers. Santos Degollado was one of these. He learned to fight and he taught others to do so, but in addition he saw to it that his men knew what they were fighting for. With a substitute president, an amateur commander, and a makeshift capital, the Constitutionalists were at a decided disadvantage. General Félix Zuloaga, who claimed the presidency for the Conservatives, had been quickly recognized by foreign governments. This made it difficult for Juárez to purchase arms and obtain credit in the United States.

To overcome this difficulty Juárez sent José-María Mata to Washington. By the summer of 1856 the Constitutionalist armies had made several notable gains. The United States, however, wanted a concession for a railroad line across the Isthmus of Tehuantepec as the price for recognition. The American government finally decided to recognize Juárez in April, 1859.

Santos Degollado marched to the gates of Mexico City, but could not force them. General Leonardo Márquez fell unexpectedly on his rear and scattered his army. After the battle General Miguel Miramón sent Márques an order to shoot his prisoners, as often happened. Later, Miramón claimed his order was limited to deserters. At any rate Márquez made it a massacre, and had the wounded dragged from their hospital beds to be shot along with doctors and medical students and volunteers who were caring for them. Though there had been many atrocities committed, this one caused a tremendous outcry, and many Conservatives withdrew their support.

Santos Degollado coolly rallied the remnants of his army in Morelia. Finding it difficult to reorganize his army and restore his reputation, he hastened to Veracruz to seek aid of Juárez. At this time Juárez decided to issue the Reform Laws.

The first of these was a decree of July 12, 1859, that nationalized Church property. Others were separation of Church and State and the establishment of civil control over the registration of marriages, births, and deaths. The Reform Laws were an effort to carry out the aims of the Constitution of 1857 and to liberate the state from the power of the clergy.

General Jesús González Ortega rose to replace Santos Degollado, and he fought his way into Mexico City in December, 1860. Juárez and his family were in Veracruz attending a performance of *Les Huguenots,* an opera about the sixteenth-century religious wars in France. Juárez rose and read the message telling that the war had ended in victory. The opera cast sang the "Marseillaise," and the crowd poured out to celebrate. On January 11, 1861, Juárez entered Mexico City in triumph.

Mexico was a shambles. There was no trade, and little in the way of agricultural production. Customs duties had been pledged for years. The victorious army had to be paid or the troubles were not yet over, and there were still small Conservative armies in remote places. The difficulties in 1861 were worse than in any of the previous years.

One tragedy followed another. Melchor Ocampo, who had long been one of Juárez' most gifted advisers, went to his home state of Michoacán, where Conservative General Márquez shot him in cold blood. Santos Degollado tried to avenge his friend's murder, and met the same fate.

Conservative refugees in France persuaded Napoleon III to establish a monarchy in Mexico under a European prince. Using the excuse of Mexican debts to French citizens, he sent an army to occupy Veracruz and collect customs duties. Spain and England, who also had debts to collect, sent token forces. As soon as they saw what the French planned, they withdrew. The French force landed on January 7, 1862.

From Mexico City Juárez declared: "To proclaim, as our adversaries do, that they are not making war upon a country, but upon its government, is to repeat the empty declaration of all those who undertake a war of aggression. . . . I shall wage . . . the war which the whole nation has accepted. . . ."

The French army marched to Puebla, which was defended by Mexican troops armed with muskets the British had used against Napoleon in the Battle of Waterloo almost half a century earlier. On May 5, 1862, the French attacked and suffered a costly defeat. Napoleon III, who planned to install a puppet emperor in Mexico, sent a much larger army. It starved out the garrison of Puebla, and marched on to Mexico City. Juárez and his cabinet fled north in his old black coach. He stopped in San Luis Potosí, less than a hundred miles from the capital.

Juárez was certain of eventual success, and his determination never wavered, even though others gave up the struggle and joined the French. Even after two years of campaigning the French army could control only the area around Mexico City. Napoleon III determined to make Maximilian of Austria Emperor of Mexico. Maximilian would not accept unless the Mexican people desired him. The forces of the Conservatives marched from town to town, demanding to know if anyone opposed Maximilian. Faced with an overwhelming force, those who opposed Maximilian remained silent. He was told that a national plebiscite had been held and that Mexicans unanimously desired him. Unfortunately for him and for Mexico, Maximilian believed this fiction. On May 28, 1864, he and his wife, Carlota, landed at Veracruz, as Mexico's Emperor and Empress.

Maximilian would have found much ground for agreement with Juárez, but he was much too liberal for the Church and the Conservatives of Mexico. He alienated the clergy by allowing a civil-marriage ceremony in the national palace. Worse than this, however, was his failure to restore to the Church lands it had been forced to sell. Maximilian was not in favor of restoring this property, but he could not have restored it if he had wished. Much Church property had been purchased by Frenchmen, and Maximilian's protector was Napoleon III, Emperor of France.

A French force marched against San Luis Potosí, and the black coach rolled northward ahead of it, out of reach. Juárez stopped in Saltillo, for Santiago Vidaurri, the *caudillo* of nearby Monterrey, was of doubtful loyalty. Vidaurri ruled the states of Coahuila and Nuevo León as his own independent domain. He invited the French to come, and defied Juárez. Juárez marched into Monterrey with his army, while the blustering *caudillo* galloped for the Texas border.

In Monterrey, Juárez received a letter from Maximilian, an invitation to meet him and discuss their differences. Juárez replied with politeness but a touch of irony: "You tell me that, abandoning the succession to a throne in Europe, forsaking your family, your friends, your fortune, and what is most dear to a man, your country, you have come with your wife, Doña Carlota, to distant and unknown lands to satisfy the summons spontaneously made by a people that rest their felicity and their future in you. I am amazed, on the one hand, by your generosity, and on the other, my surprise has been great to read in your letter the words *spontaneous summons,* for I had already perceived that when traitors of my country appeared at Miramar as a self-constituted commission to offer you the Crown of Mexico . . . you saw in all this merely a ridiculous farce, unworthy of serious consideration by any honorable and self-respecting man. . . . I am forced to conclude for lack of time, and I shall merely add one more remark. It is given to men, sir, to attack the rights of others, to take their property, to attempt the lives of those who defend their liberty, and to make of their virtues a crime and of their own vices a virtue; but there is one thing which is beyond the reach of perversity, and that is the tremendous verdict of history. History will judge us. I am your obedient servant, Benito Juárez."

One of the French officers, General du Barail, was leaving for France when Maximilian arrived. He had already become badly disillusioned by the French intervention in Mexico. "Poor Maximilian! I thought. What are you going to do . . . amid those people who have been tearing one another apart for more than forty years; in the thick of those intrigues fed by fanaticism and greed . . . in this Mexico without trade or industry; in this Mexico which has been killed by its mining wealth, leaving civil war the only possible branch of human activity . . . ? The very defenders of your throne, those Mexicans who have called you, will abandon you, because you cannot go through with their retro-grade plans. . . . If you succeed in bringing order out of this chaos, prosperity out of this poverty, and union into these hearts, you will be the greatest sovereign of modern times. But I very much fear that the task you have undertaken is above human strength. Poor fool! You will regret your fine castle of Miramar."

These were prophetic words, for though Maximilian was kind and well meaning, his rule in Mexico was a catalogue of failures. Even so, the Liberal cause often appeared hopeless. Marshal Bazaine sent troops against Monterrey and drove Juárez and his government into the northern desert. For a time Juárez remained in El Paso. He refused to leave Mexico, however, for that would signify a victory for his enemies.

Many countries of South America celebrated Juárez in his time of trials. Colombia, for example, called him *Benemérito de América* (Well-deserving of America), and placed his portrait in the National Library. He wrote to his family, "I am grateful for this favor, but it does not go to my head because I know that I do not deserve so much eulogy. I have simply tried to do my duty and nothing else."

The rumor spread that Juárez had crossed the border to seek refuge in the United States. Maximilian believed it, and he was persuaded that the way to pacify the country completely was to issue a severe decree, outlawing all the resistance bands and authorizing the death penalty for all who were captured. This decree of October 3, 1865, shocked all of Mexico and many foreign countries. The struggle now became a war to the death, with no prisoners being taken by either side. This did not change drastically what had unofficially been the practice, but it made the practice known to the world. The United States Secretary of State protested to the French Foreign Minister.

Many of the patriots wearied of the struggle, and abandoned Juárez, but others came to take their places. Juárez gave no sign of grief. "Better alone than in bad company," was his only comment.

When the American Civil War ended, both President Andrew

Johnson and Secretary of State Seward suggested to Napoleon III that he withdraw his troops from Mexico. Concerned also about the rapid rise of Prussia, Napoleon agreed to recall his army. He urged Maximilian to prepare to carry on with Mexican troops. A Belgian officer in Mexico wrote, "The day that the French army sails, the Empire will collapse with a bang." Carlota sailed for France to persuade Napoleon III to continue his military support.

Maximilian planned to abdicate, but was urged to remain. The Mexican Conservatives were especially anxious for him to stay, so that all blame for the intervention could be heaped on him. Napoleon III later urged him to abdicate, but he wanted no advice from Paris after Napoleon withdrew his support. His mother wrote him that he must not leave with the baggage of the French army. Pride made him decide to remain in Mexico until he could leave with fitting dignity. Carlota also urged him to stay. After being rebuffed in Paris, she traveled to Rome, to seek papal support. The Pope reminded her of Maximilian's failure to restore Church lands. Carlota went insane, but lived on in Belgium until 1926.

Before departing, the French tried to make some agreement with Juárez. As one officer wrote: "Juárez is not the man who has been so decried in France, he is a Mexican and has many of the defects of his race undoubtedly, but few of his countrymen have so many qualities. He is disinterested, he is ready to efface himself if the interests of his country so demand, he is anything but bloodthirsty. . . ." Napoleon III, however, could not bring himself to make a treaty with Juárez, as this would signify that he had been defeated.

On February 5, 1867, the French army marched out of Mexico City for Veracruz and France. The patriots began their march toward the capital. At Zacatecas, General Miramón counterattacked. Juárez sent his carriage along the road to Fresnillo and rode out with the cavalry. Miramón saw the old black coach, and his cavalry captured it, but the prize had escaped. When Zacatecas was recovered, the patriots found an order signed by Maximilian to try Juárez and his ministers by court-martial, but to refer the sentence to him before executing it. No one could be sure what Maximilian intended to do, but it seemed clear that he would let Juárez be shot.

From Zacatecas the patriots fought their way toward the capital. Maximilian joined his army at Querétaro, where they were besieged from February to May, 1867. With his generals Miramón, Méndez, Márquez, and Mexía, Maximilian completed the "Five Tragic M's."

On May 15th General Escobedo's men captured Maximilian, who informed his captors that he had abdicated, and he asked for an escort to Veracruz. When he learned that he was to be tried by a military court, he protested and requested an interview with Juárez. Juárez, knowing of Maximilian's personal charm and magnetism, stayed at San Luis Potosí, while Maximilian remained at Querétaro.

The trial lasted three days. Maximilian's lawyers, though they were Liberals, nevertheless made a spirited effort to save his life. They pointed out that Jefferson Davis had not been executed after the Civil War. Many men and women came to Juárez to plead with him to spare Maximilian's life. "The government acts by necessity on this occasion," he said, "denying the humanitarian sentiments of which it has given and will still give innumerable proofs. The law and the sentence are inexorable now, because public safety so demands."

Diplomats, by the score, the Princess Salm-Salm, a delegation of two hundred women, and the wife of Miramón, all called on Juárez and begged him to spare Maximilian. Victor Hugo wrote him from France. Garibaldi, who was popular in Mexico, also wrote in behalf of Maximilian. Juárez and his government remained firm. The law must be upheld; Europeans must learn that they could not violate Mexico's rights with impunity. Too many Mexicans remembered the scores of patriots who had been shot out of hand by authority of Maximilian's decree of October 3rd. If mercy was so valued, where was it hiding when he was in power?

Maximilian remained serene to the end, and said not one word against Juárez. Though Juárez refused to see him, he wrote: "May my blood be the last to be shed, and devote that perseverance which you have shown in defending the cause that has just triumphed, and which I was glad to recognize and esteem in prosperity, to the nobler task of reconciling souls and founding peace in this unfortunate country." It is one of the ironies of history that Juárez and Maximilian, who shared many of the same views, should be antagonists. After Maximilian was shot by a firing squad it was said of him that he knew better how to die than how to rule.

On July 17, 1867, Juárez wearily entered the capital once more. Mexico had been battered and torn after the War of the Reform. She was not only more battered than ever now, but also burdened with the tremendous debts piled up by the imperial regime. The Empire was no more, but the Republic still had to pay for it.

An election was held, and Juárez won over Porfirio Díaz, who was one of the patriot generals, and over Sebastián Lerdo de Tejada, one of his ministers. Juárez cut down the size of the Army drastically to save money. Many of the officers and soldiers were resentful, for they had conquered the country, and felt that it was theirs by right. Small-scale military revolts broke out, though Díaz did not take part in them. Instead, he returned to Oaxaca, collected a store of weapons, and waited.

In 1871, when the presidential term ended, Juárez was exhausted and ill. The death of his wife early in this same year was a blow from which he did not recover completely. Juárez nevertheless announced his candidacy, and Díaz and Sebastián Lerdo campaigned again. No candidate won a majority of the votes. Congress was left to make the final choice, and it chose Juárez, on October 12, 1871.

Juárez had suffered a heart attack the previous year. On July 18, 1872, he was struck again, and this time the attack was fatal. In his last hours Juárez remained the stoic Zapotec Indian he had been all his life. His plans for developing Mexico economically and politically were still far from fulfilled. But at least, owing largely to his leadership, Mexico had finally become a nation.

Porfirio Díaz
1830–1915

José de la Cruz Porfirio Díaz was born in the city of Oaxaca in Mexico. He was baptized on September 15th, probably within a few days of his birth. His father presumably was a Spaniard or Creole, and his mother was a mestiza, half Spanish and half Mixteca Indian. In 1833 his father died, and the family had a difficult time. Porfirio was able to get some primary school education, and he learned the carpenter's trade. When he was fifteen, he entered the seminary to study for the priesthood.

During the War between Mexico and the United States a militia unit of boys was formed in Oaxaca, and Díaz thus gained some military training. In hope of being able to take an active part in the war, he walked to Mexico City, but arrived too late. He returned to complete his courses at the seminary in 1849, but the priestly calling had no appeal for him. He turned instead to law, and attended lectures given by Benito Juárez.

In 1854 Santa Anna exiled Juárez. In January of that year the Liberals had proclaimed the Plan de Ayutla, for the purpose of deposing the tyrant and establishing constitutional rule. Santa Anna called for a vote in which Mexicans were to declare for him or against him. Díaz boldly voted against Santa Anna, then galloped out of town before he could be arrested. He joined a partisan band of Liberals.

The Plan de Ayutla, in addition to calling for the overthrow of Santa Anna, was an attempt to end the privileges of the Church and the Army. These joined forces in the defense of their privileged position, and attempted to make the Liberal cause appear to be an attack on religion. Santa Anna was forced into exile, nevertheless, and the Liberals took over the government. Juárez became president of the Supreme Court and Minister of Justice.

After the Liberals promulgated their Constitution of 1857, the War of the Reform began. The Conservatives seized the capital, and President Ignacio Comonfort fled the country. As the constitution had abolished the office of vice president, Juárez was next in line in the succession, and he assumed the leadership of the Liberal cause. Díaz became one of the ablest and most active of the Liberal officers.

Juárez sent Díaz south to Tehuantepec to win control of the region. He could spare only 150 men and no money, but Díaz soon raised an army and sent captured money to Juárez. Díaz, by his achievements, won two promotions, to major and then to lieutenant colonel. By the end of 1859 he had been raised to colonel. In 1860 the Liberals fought their way into Mexico City, and Díaz became a deputy in the new Congress.

The Church was now forced to sell its vast properties except for those buildings used for worship. The Ley Lerdo, which prohibited corporations from owning property, was aimed solely at the Church, but it was soon used to deprive the Indian communities of their communal lands. The Church, meanwhile, found a new champion in General Leonardo Márquez, an Indian from Querétaro. In June of 1861 Márquez attacked the capital while Congress was in session. Díaz left his seat in the chamber and joined in the repulse of the Conservative army.

Mexico was in a state of near exhaustion after the War of the Reform. Mexican Conservative exiles in France whetted the appetite of ambitious Napoleon III by talking of the ease with which France could intervene in Mexico. In 1861 the American Civil War was beginning, and the time seemed ripe for taking over Mexico. England, France, and Spain sent troops to Veracruz, presumably to collect debts owed their countrymen. When the English and Spanish perceived the French intentions to occupy Mexico, they withdrew.

Juárez sent General Ignacio Zaragoza to oppose the French,

and Díaz was a brigadier general under him. French Zouaves and Chasseurs easily forced their way through one of the mountain passes weakly held by Indian conscripts. The French general naturally assumed that all Mexican troops could be scattered by a charge. Zaragoza withdrew to Puebla and prepared to fight. His troops were posted behind heavy stone walls.

The French marched scornfully against the town, and were treated to a bloodbath. Díaz added to the destruction by slipping out with a party of men and attacking the French flank. Later he admitted that "the victory was so unexpected we were surprised . . . by it. . . ." However, the French had so impressed their foes with their ability and courage, that Zaragoza did not even try to pursue them.

Juárez now sent all available men to hold Puebla, while the French brought new forces from Europe. In May of 1863 a French army of 26,000 men closed in on Puebla to starve the garrison out. Díaz urged the commander, General Jesús González Ortega, to send out troops to harass the French at strategic points, but González Ortega refused.

During the two-month siege Díaz played a prominent role, and his fame spread throughout Mexico. When Puebla fell, he and some other officers escaped to join Juárez in Mexico City. Since he had no army with which to oppose the French, Juárez moved his government north to San Luis Potosí. Díaz, now a general of a division, was sent to Querétaro to raise an army. While Juárez was in the northern deserts, Díaz marched to Oaxaca with the Army of the East. The governor, Cajiga, who had supported Maximilian, was far from happy to see him, and asked if he intended to use force. Díaz had learned that ferocious language sometimes made harsh measures unnecessary. What he said to the governor is not known, but the governor mounted a swift horse and left for Mexico City. Díaz took over his post.

The French could not advance against Oaxaca without building a road over which to haul supplies and cannons. They employed the last months of 1864 and the early ones of 1865 in road building. When the road was completed, they attacked the city.

Díaz had worked hard at fortifying Oaxaca, but most of his troops deserted to join Maximilian's armies. This was the low point in the resistance to the French. General Uraga, who abandoned his friends to join the French, wrote Díaz and urged him to follow. Díaz refused, and held Oaxaca until his small force was overpowered. He was sent to Puebla as a prisoner of war.

Two months later the American Civil War ended, and it was clear that Napoleon III had miscalculated in expecting a Confederate victory. Díaz waited quietly at Puebla, for the French could not remain much longer in Mexico without risking a clash with the United States. At this time the United States had the most powerful army in the world.

In September, Díaz escaped, and gradually built up an army of followers. By 1866 he controlled the southeast, and had set up a government and a treasury. Men were beginning to look on him as a statesman, above the crowd of opportunists who changed sides as easily as they changed uniforms.

The French began their withdrawal, leaving Maximilian dependent upon Mexican troops. Díaz led 2,000 enemy troops into a trap by pretending to flee, then surrounded them. After the battle he ordered many of the captured officers to be shot by firing squads, in retaliation for earlier executions of captured Liberals.

The enemy fell back to Oaxaca, and Díaz stationed his troops around the town. He learned from a captured messenger that help for the enemy was coming. He decided to intercept the relief column. He had noticed earlier that his plans were known to the enemy soon after he announced them, so he told a number of individuals that he intended to attack a certain section of Oaxaca the next night. The enemy mounted a heavy guard and waited for the attack. When the sun rose they saw that Díaz had withdrawn his entire force. He captured the relief column, and soon afterward Oaxaca surrendered to him.

In February, 1867, the last of the French troops embarked at Veracruz. Maximilian unwisely chose to stay on and fight, though his cause was obviously hopeless. Early in April, Díaz took Puebla, and on June 20th he entered Mexico City, the day after

Maximilian had been executed in Querétaro. Porfirio Díaz' political career now began. He stood before his countrymen as a successful soldier who did not change sides or betray his nation.

When he entered Mexico City, Díaz was careful to use only his most disciplined troops. By this action he saved the city from pillage and massacre, and the inhabitants were grateful. In Mexican conflicts the conquerors too often behaved like pirates, and ordinarily showed no mercy to those who had opposed them. By his actions Díaz set himself apart.

When Juárez arrived, Díaz turned over to him the large sum of money he had collected in his campaigns, then resigned his command. He declared later that Juárez had been cool toward him since the siege of Puebla. Juárez recognized in Díaz an able and ambitious rival for power, and he did not intend to encourage competition for control of Mexico.

After his resignation Díaz returned to his native Oaxaca, where his grateful countrymen gave him a plantation called La Noria (The Waterwheel). Here he applied himself to the raising of sugar cane. His friends, as well as the enemies of Juárez, frequently visited him. He was not allowed to forget politics, nor did he intend to. The time was not ripe for him to act, and he was too wise to overplay his hand.

In 1867 Juárez was elected president, in reward for his perseverance against the French. He had been acting president during that time, and the nation generally conceded that he deserved the presidency.

When Juárez ran again in 1871, however, it was a different matter, for the constitution did not allow immediate re-election. Juárez felt that the nation's perilous condition required his personal leadership. Díaz and Sebastián Lerdo de Tejada campaigned against him. No one received a majority of votes. Congress had to choose the president, and its choice was Juárez.

Three weeks later the *porfiristas* (followers of Porfirio Díaz) rebelled. Loyal troops pacified Oaxaca, while Díaz moved to Zacatecas, north of Mexico City. Government troops marched on Zacatecas, but Díaz eluded them and led a column of cavalry to

Mexico City, in hope that the people would rise in his favor. He found no support, and had to withdraw. Then, on July 8th, Juárez died.

Lerdo became provisional president and temporarily won the loyalty of the former Juárez supporters. Once more Díaz returned to Oaxaca to bide his time. He was by no means through with politics, for he felt that Lerdo's popularity would not last. Lerdo was soon unpopular even with his own followers.

In the elections of 1875 Díaz came out of retirement once more, and this time he was determined to gain the presidency. He arranged for an uprising in Oaxaca, then sailed to Brownsville, Texas. The rebellion in Oaxaca succeeded, and other uprisings occurred in many places. Díaz sailed to Veracruz and made his way to Oaxaca. He soon defeated Lerdo's army, and most of the troops were quite willing to join him. Lerdo fled into exile. In 1878 Díaz became president, to serve until 1880, when Lerdo's term would have ended.

In his first speech to the Congress, Díaz insisted that the Army be rewarded, for he knew its support was essential. This meant prompt payment of the troops and restoration of pensions halted earlier for lack of funds. The treasury was still empty, but Díaz knew that no Mexican government could stay long in power if the Army was dissatisfied.

When Díaz took over the government, Mexico had behind her half a century of suffering. The presidency had been the plaything of adventurers like Santa Anna, and only a few rare individuals like Juárez had been truly dedicated to serving the nation. Endless conflict had ruined the country economically, and the future was still bleak. Díaz was hard pressed to meet any of the government's financial obligations, but he quickly informed foreign governments that Mexico would somehow meet her responsibilities. This action gave him relief from the danger of foreign intervention, but did not solve his problems.

Mexico swarmed with bandits, and there was little law enforcement anywhere. No road was safe for travel. To pacify Mexico was an enormous task, but Díaz knew that it must be done. There could be no travel or commerce until the roads were made safe. He organized the *rurales,* a rural police force with authority to impose summary justice.

Many of the rurales were recruited from among the bandits, for they were skillful fighters who did not shrink from shedding blood, and they knew all the roads and hideouts. Díaz made them a simple offer—*Pan ó palo* (Bread or the club). Those who joined were given handsome uniforms and high-peaked sombreros, and they rode the best horses available. Those who refused the offer were tracked down and shot by ex-bandits who knew their ways.

The rurales employed harsh methods. They frequently invoked what was called the *ley fuga,* or law of flight. When courts and jails were far away, prisoners were a nuisance. The rurales simply took their prisoners out of sight of witnesses and shot them. The excuse was that they were "attempting to escape."

Because of the severe financial straits of the country, Díaz reduced his own salary almost by half, and taxed civil officials on their salaries. He was careful to see that salaries were paid regularly, and in this fashion lessened the discontent. The tax on salaries remained in effect until 1896, when it was no longer needed.

In addition to pacifying the country, Díaz also had to restore the economy and maintain friendly relations with the United States. It required enormous energy and unusual ability to meet these problems. Díaz knew his countrymen well, and how to deal with them. Because he also proved able in his diplomatic relations with other governments, he was respected abroad as well as at home.

Juárez had planned to lead Mexico along the paths of democratic and economic development at the same time. Díaz concentrated on maintaining peace and developing the economy, but he had little use for democracy or representative government. The governor of Veracruz captured some supposed *Lerdista* plotters, and wired Díaz for instructions. In his famous Veracruz Telegram Díaz made this terse reply: "If you catch them in the act, kill them in cold blood." The governor quickly executed the alleged plotters along with nine of his personal enemies who were not involved in the conspiracy. By this act Díaz made it known that plotting against the government was a dangerous game.

Because he had protested the re-election of Juárez, Díaz felt obliged to step down at the end of his first term. He allowed General Manuel González, a trusted but inept comrade, to serve as president. González regarded the presidency as a reward for military service, and his administration was thoroughly corrupt. There was no danger of González becoming a rival for the presidency.

González recklessly granted concessions for the building of railroads, and he authorized certain companies to make surveys of public lands. These companies received as payment one-third of the area they surveyed. Many Indian villages were looted of their lands. When they resisted, the rurales killed the men and shipped the women and children off to labor on the tropical plantations of Quintana Roo.

The land surveys were followed by sales of vast tracts of land to friends of the government—generals, politicians, and American investors. Mexico thus gave up control of about one-quarter of her national territory. Concentration of landownership was greatly increased, for a few hundred families and companies owned most of the land fit for cultivation. Seventeen individuals acquired ninety-six million acres, about one-fifth of Mexico.

When Díaz was elected to succeed González, Mexico was again on the verge of ruin, and it took strenuous efforts to save the country from bankruptcy. Díaz was aided by Romero Rubio, who had served as Minister of the Treasury under Lerdo. In 1881 Díaz married Carmen Rubio, Romero's daughter. The Rubios were one of Mexico's most prominent families, and under their influence Díaz began wearing a frock coat and top hat. His wife persuaded him to relax the laws against the Church, which once more acquired both property and political influence. In other countries at this time the Church began supporting social reforms, but it did not do so in Mexico owing to its relationship with Díaz. It thus lost the opportunity of identifying itself with the Mexican people rather than with their rulers. After 1910 the Church would pay a high price for this arrangement, for it was regarded as a partner of the dictatorship and an enemy of the people.

Potential rivals of Díaz usually met sudden death or went into exile. Presidential ambition, said the Mexicans, was a fatal disease. Divide and rule was Díaz' policy, and he skillfully kept his opponents from uniting. He extended his control over the state governors, so that they also became agents of his rule. Congress was so subservient to his wishes that he scornfully referred to it as *mi caballada* (my horse herd). He presented lists of those he wanted elected to Congress. Occasionally these lists contained the names of men who had died. It made no difference—they were elected anyway.

The courts, too, fell under complete control. According to his wishes, foreigners involved in lawsuits received favorable verdicts. Wealthy Mexicans, if they were friendly to Díaz, also were kindly treated by the courts. For the poor, however, "justice" was a term that had no meaning. If they resisted any outrage against them, they were quickly and brutally punished, by the *ley fuga* or by slow death on the tropical plantations of Quintana Roo and Oaxaca.

Because his rule brought both relative domestic peace in place of anarchy and economic development where little had existed before, Díaz won the support of Mexican intellectuals. What he was doing, they reasoned, was badly needed. If his methods were harsh, it was only because mild methods would have failed.

The looting of Indian lands under González and Díaz deprived villages of lands they had held since before the coming of Cortez. Thousands of Indians were displaced or shot or sent as virtual slaves to Yucatán because friends of Díaz or of the state governors coveted their lands. The most flagrant case of all was that of the Yaquis of Sonora, who waged a bitter war to protect their lands. When they finally surrendered, they were sold to the planters of Quintana Roo for seventy-five pesos apiece. Díaz did not order this "Second Conquest," but he permitted it.

Díaz was especially concerned with the state of the national treasury. He was convinced that every man had a price, and, as he put it, a dog with a bone neither kills nor steals. His view of his countrymen was cynical, but the actions of many of them seemed to justify his attitude toward them. In 1893 he appointed José Ives Limantour, an able man of French descent, as Secretary of the Treasury. In the next year, for the first time since independence, the treasury had a surplus rather than a deficit.

Limantour was the spokesman of a new group of powerful men, the *científicos*. They were wedded to the positivism of Auguste Comte, and the material development was their primary goal. They wanted to see Mexico dominated by a white élite and developed by foreign capital. They believed in honest and efficient government, for they disliked petty graft. Many of them became millionaires through large-scale financial operations involving government funds.

Until the rise of the *científicos* Díaz had never completely lost a feeling of attachment to the Indians and mestizos among whom he had lived as a youth. He had occasionally intervened to protect Indian villages. But the *científicos* regarded Indians as mere brutes fit only for menial labor. From 1895 on, their views strongly flavored the administration. By this time Díaz was an old man, completely out of touch with the people he ruled, but still convinced that his rule was benevolent.

From a distance it appeared that Díaz had indeed accomplished a miracle. Mexican roads were the safest in the world—for foreigners. Statistics showed the country to be prosperous. Mexico's credit abroad was high, and foreign investors were delighted with the profits they made and the protection they received. Some 9,000 miles of railroad tracks had been laid, and telegraph lines extended in all directions. Mexico City was adorned by expensive public buildings and palatial private homes.

In the towns and cities were about 12,000 schools, which contributed to the growing literacy of the urban population. The countryside, however, remained virtually unchanged. Poverty and hunger were widespread. The dictatorship's hold on the country seemed unbreakable, and there was little reason for hope.

Land hunger had become acute in Mexico, for more than half of Mexican land was owned by less than 3,000 families. Of the ten million who worked on the land, less than half a million owned any land at all. The peons' wages remained unchanged while prices rose steadily. By 1910 the peons were in a desperate condition, for their wages would buy only one-fourth as much as they had a century earlier.

Resentment against foreign capitalists was rising, for the wealth produced by Mexican mines and oil fields was for the benefit of aliens. Under Díaz, Mexico had become "the stepmother of Mexicans." In trying to attract foreign investors Díaz had neglected to protect Mexican interests, so that nearly all technicians and administrators were foreigners. To please investors Díaz provided a cheap and docile labor supply. Mexicans who dared to organize unions and to strike for higher pay were shot down by order of their own government.

In yet another way Díaz served his countrymen ill, for he refused to prepare his successor. He had never allowed rivals to rise in the past, and he did not change his ways as his eightieth birthday approached. There were potential successors, such as General Bernardo Reyes and Limantour, but Díaz diverted attention from them.

By 1904 many Mexicans were concerned over the question of the succession. To quiet their fears Díaz permitted Congress to restore the office of vice president at the same time that it extended the president's term to six years. Díaz chose Ramón Corral for vice president, and he was duly elected. Corral was best known for the fortune he made selling Yaqui captives when he was governor of Sonora. No one would want to oust Díaz in favor of Corral.

In 1908 Díaz told an American journalist that he intended to retire in 1910 and that he would welcome an opposition party. This statement was for foreign consumption, but young Mexican intellectuals believed it and began to talk of reform. The followers of General Reyes became active, and Díaz sent Reyes on a mission abroad, a polite form of exile.

The need for a leader was so great and the sentiment for change so strong, however, that Díaz was to be toppled from power by the least likely of all possible foes—Francisco I. Madero. A member of a wealthy hacendado family of Chihuahua, Madero was small of stature, squeaky of voice, a spiritualist, and a vegetarian. Educated abroad, he had developed humanitarian ideals. He had tried to improve living conditions for the peons on his family's estates. Díaz was not alone in regarding Madero as odd.

In 1908 Madero wrote a little book, called *The Presidential Succession in 1910,* that propelled him to the center of the political arena. In it he accepted the fact that Díaz would be elected president, but mildly suggested that Mexicans be allowed to choose the vice president. The followers of Reyes turned to Madero, and nominated him for the presidency.

At first Díaz was amused at the spectacle of a little man with a high-pitched voice and a nervous tic campaigning against him. When he learned of the huge crowds that turned out to cheer Madero, his smile faded. To be on the safe side he had Madero imprisoned in San Luis Potosí until after the election. As was to be expected, Díaz and Corral won easily. When released, Madero crossed the border into Texas, and proclaimed his Plan de San Luis Potosí, declaring the election void and calling for a general revolt.

The Mexican Revolution was thus timidly launched, and it appeared at first to be nothing serious. Madero crossed into Coahuila, where he was told an army awaited him. He found a dozen armed men and an equal number of unarmed ones, and quickly returned to Texas. Greatly discouraged, he traveled to New Orleans and prepared to sail for Europe. At this time he learned that Pascual Orozco and Pancho Villa had defeated federal troops. In February, 1911, he returned to lead the movement. There were outbreaks all over Mexico, and Díaz called Limantour back from Europe, where he had gone in anger at being deprived of the vice presidency.

Limantour took charge of the government and agreed to introduce reforms. He sent for Bernardo Reyes, and opened negotiations with the rebels. Madero probably would have been easy to persuade, but his family and other rebel leaders refused to listen. On May 25, 1911, Díaz and Limantour bowed to the inevitable, and resigned.

Once he had resigned, Díaz was not molested in any way or shown any disrespect. Bewildered at the ingratitude of his people, he boarded the train for Veracruz and left for Europe. He lived in Paris until his death on July 2, 1915. Mexico was still torn by bitter and bloody strife. Madero and his vice president, Pino Suárez, had been shot "by friends attempting to rescue them," according to official report. Watching the terrible destruction of life and property convinced Díaz that his way of governing Mexico had been the right one. He apparently never understood the depths to which he had pushed the Mexican masses, or their powerful hunger for land. Nor did he admit that the destruction might have been prevented if he had been willing to arrange for a peaceful succession.

The debate over the merits and demerits of the dictatorship still goes on, for it is a many-sided problem. It is true that Díaz established law and order and that otherwise nothing at all could have been accomplished. It is also true that he continued the plans of Juárez for economic development and that the Mexican economy was transformed during his long rule. But he abandoned the Juárez program for political and social development, and in these matters there was serious retrogression. The vaunted economic development, furthermore, benefitted only foreigners and a few privileged Mexicans, while it weighed heavily and painfully on the majority of Mexican workingmen. The Mexican Revolution was fought to undo much of what the Díaz régime had done to Mexico. Out of this struggle came a Mexican determination that no similar régime should ever arise again. In the final analysis, this attitude is perhaps the best measure of the Díaz régime in the eyes of the majority of the Mexican people.

PART VI

Three Argentines

Bartolomé Mitre's life spanned most of the nineteenth century, and his activities were equally far-reaching and extensive. He was soldier and statesman, journalist and scholar, and Argentina's grand old man. He represents the second generation of Argentine liberals. He was present, if not a participant, when most of the important events of the nineteenth century occurred, from independence to the end of the century.

Irigoyen represents another phase of Argentine political development, the rise to power of the middle-class Radical party. He was the first president of humble birth, the first that was not acceptable to the landed oligarchy. Unfortunately for Argentina, Irigoyen's administration floundered hopelessly in the depths of the Great Depression, and its fall in 1930 carried down with it respect for democracy and representative government. Thirty-five years later Argentina still has not been able to return to the course followed by Mitre.

One of the reasons Argentina strayed so far from her familiar path was the interlude of Juan and Evita Perón. This couple captured the imagination of the Argentine masses, and for a brief period they shone brilliantly as an astute political team. Evita was a modern version of the Cinderella story, and Perón was her Prince Charming. Together they had a tremendous opportunity to aid in the development of their country and its people, an opportunity they failed to take. They did make organized labor aware of its political strength, but they used labor for selfish purposes of their own. As a result of their meteoric rise and fall, Argentina is still floundering, with frequent changes of government, an empty treasury, and chronic inflation.

Bartolomé Mitre
1821–1906

The year before Bartolomé Mitre was born was the "Terrible Year '20" in Argentina. In that fatal year the province was in a state of anarchy, and there was no national government at all. Mitre's mother was Josefa Martínez Wetherton, half Irish and half Spanish. He was born in Buenos Aires, and therefore was a porteño by birth.

When Mitre was a boy of ten years his father, Don Ambrosio, sent him to work for one of the major ranchers, Don Gervasio Rosas, brother of Juan Manuel de Rosas, Argentina's most famous tyrant (1835–1852). He learned all the tasks performed on a large cattle ranch. His father undoubtedly hoped that he would learn all that was needed to run a ranch and then become an *estanciero* himself. It was, perhaps, his love of books that lured Mitre away from the career of ranching.

The Rosas library proved his undoing, for he spent all possible time reading. Finally Don Gervasio sent him to a neighbor with a note. "Kindly do me the service of taking the young Mitre to his father," he wrote. "As a caballerito, he is no good; the moment he sees a little shade, he dismounts and sets to reading."

Mitre attended the Escuela Normal de Besnos Irigoyen, and after it the Escuela de Comercia del Consulado. He entered the latter school in 1835, the same year Juan Manuel de Rosas began his dictatorship of Buenos Aires province. Even before this time Mitre's family had moved to Montevideo, where his father had

Benito Juárez (1806-1872)
An Indian president and defender of Mexico.

Porfirio Díaz (1830-1915)
For thirty years the absolute ruler of modern Mexico.

Bartolomé Mitre (1821-1906)
Journalist, soldier, scholar, and statesman of Argentina.

Hipólito Irigoyen (1852-1933)
The Argentine democrat who helped kill democracy.

María Eva Duarte de Perón (1919-1952)
Argentina's working girl who made good.

been born. This was the chief refuge of the unitarists, against whom Rosas waged unrelenting war.

In 1837 Mitre's father tried to find him a suitable career in the military life. Mitre was sent to the Colegio Militar de Montevideo. During political struggles in Uruguay, the cadets were pressed into the service of General Oribe. In 1839 Mitre joined forces with General Fructuoso Rivera, and his rise was rapid thereafter.

Rivera was a *unitario* (unitarist), and therefore an enemy of Buenos Aires dictator Rosas, who was a federalist. Rosas supported Oribe in his attempt to wrest the presidency from Rivera by force. In February, 1843, after a crushing defeat in December, Rivera was besieged in Montevideo. Among the other defenders were General José María Paz, one of the ablest of Argentine officers, an Italian legion under famed Guiseppe Garibaldi, a French legion, and one from Buenos Aires. Mitre, now an artillery officer, was also active among the besieged. At the age of twenty-five he was promoted to lieutenant colonel. Much of his military knowledge was gained from General Paz. Both of them were admirers of the independence hero General San Martín, and Paz encouraged Mitre in the idea of a career of devotion to his country.

Mitre's ability and knowledge of artillery and its use were such that he was able to write a manual, *Instrucción Práctica de Artillería*, which was widely used by artillery officers. It was during the long siege that Mitre married Delfina de Vedia, daughter of a Uruguayan general.

Mitre always showed an interest in writing, and began submitting articles and poems to newspapers. He also wrote some plays, and he translated novels from other languages into Spanish. After three years of the siege, the Uruguayans became suspicious of the Argentines among them. In 1846 feelings reached a peak, and Mitre and the other Argentines had no choice but to leave. He first went up the Paraná to join General Paz, but by the time he arrived Urquiza had defeated Paz and scattered his army. Mitre went next to Brazil.

From Rio he traveled to Bolivia, sailing to the Pacific coast through the Straits of Magellan. He especially wanted to visit Bolivia to see her ancient ruins. In La Paz he was asked to serve on the Bolivian General Staff, and he soon became editor of *La Época*. In October, 1847, he was named director of the Colegio Militar of Bolivia.

In January, 1848, Mitre was obliged to leave Bolivia when rebels seized the government. He was escorted to the Peruvian border. The Peruvian government was suspicious of Bolivian exiles, and Mitre sought asylum in Chile. He was rescued from financial difficulties by a position on *El Comercio*, a paper belonging to his countryman Juan Bautista Alberdi. After Alberdi sold the paper, the new owner made Mitre sole editor. He began writing serious articles on many Chilean problems, and soon became one of the spokesmen for Chilean Liberals.

In 1851 the Liberals rebelled against the heavy-handed rule of the Conservative party. The revolt was crushed, and the government imprisoned a number of men thought to be troublemakers. Among these were Mitre and the Chilean Liberal Benjamín Vicuña-Mackenna. Mitre remained calm and good-natured. Vicuña-Mackenna simply disguised himself as a woman, and walked out. Mitre was banished to Peru, where it was expected that he would be persecuted. Chile soon granted general amnesty, however, and allowed him to return.

This time Mitre and the other Argentine exiles began serious planning for the overthrow of dictator Juan Manuel Rosas. Sarmiento suggested an invasion of his native province of San Juan. At this time, 1851, they learned that Urquiza had broken with Rosas. In September they sailed to join Urquiza, who had received financial and military aid from Brazil.

Before marching against Rosas, Urquiza marched from his province of Entre Ríos to Uruguay, and raised the siege of Montevideo, which had gone on for nearly ten years. In December, 1851, Urquiza crossed his army over the Paraná River into Santa Fe Province. In January he ordered the allied army south to battle Rosas. In February, after defeating Rosas' vanguard, Urquiza met the main enemy force at Monte Caseros. After an exchange of artillery fire, Urquiza's cavalry charged, and the Rosista army fled toward Buenos Aires.

This battle, in which Mitre commanded an artillery battalion, ended the Rosas era and marked the beginning of the modern Argentine nation. Before the smoke and dust had settled, Urquiza promoted Mitre to colonel for his valuable handling of the artillery.

Urquiza immediately granted amnesty, and tried by tactful measures to win the goodwill and cooperation of the people of Bueno Aires. He did not enter the city as a conqueror, and maintained that there were neither conquerors nor conquered. Nothing he could do, however, could dissipate the porteño opposition to him as a leader of another province. They would follow no one but a porteño. Buenos Aires, they felt, was vastly superior to any other Argentine city, and she deserved a superior position in relation to back-country provinces and cities. The porteños were unyielding on this point, and there could be no real national unity until the problem was solved.

Urquiza called elections for a provincial assembly, and Mitre was one of the delegates elected. Mitre founded a daily paper, *Los Debates*, in order to publicize his views. He soon began opposing Urquiza's policies, and thereby raised his own popularity in Buenos Aires.

Probably the most crucial problem concerned the location of the capital. As long as the city of Buenos Aires was a part of the province of Buenos Aires, and not a federal district, the customs duties collected belonged to the province and city, and not to the nation. It was on this issue that Urquiza had finally broken with Rosas, for all other provinces were virtually paying tribute to Buenos Aires.

In the 1820's Bernardino Rivadavia had tried to solve this problem by federalizing the city, but it was only a temporary measure. The porteños were violently opposed to this solution, logical and fair though it might be, and Urquiza dropped the matter rather than drive the porteños to armed resistance. He called a meeting of provincial governors, and asked them for advice on designing a plan for union. They drew up articles of government to serve until a constitution had been adopted for the Argentine Confederation.

In Buenos Aires there was general opposition to the agreement, and Mitre was the first to speak against it. He attacked it principally for giving too much power to Urquiza. He reminded the porteños of the Rosas tyranny. Since the constitution was to be the product of combined efforts of all the provinces, Mitre's charge that the national government would be a dictatorship seems only a means to defeat plans for a government in which Buenos Aires would share power equally with other provinces. Mitre was a genuine lover of liberty, but he was also a porteño.

Urquiza, who had been restrained in his actions, and who had made no threatening gestures or uses of his extraordinary powers, was puzzled. He was camped outside the city with an army, yet he refrained from using it or even hinting at its use. When the opposition was most intense and mobs surrounded the legislative hall, he rode up to its doors alone and unguarded. Meanwhile Mitre organized a provincial militia, and prepared for revolt.

Urquiza was in Santa Fe when the revolt occurred. Knowing that unity could never be achieved by force, he withdrew all of the Confederation's troops from the province. The Argentine Confederation proceeded to organize a government without the province of Buenos Aires.

Mitre was given charge of defense of the province, and called for volunteers. In three days 4,000 men answered the call. Urquiza went ahead with plans for drawing up a constitution, and repeated the invitation to Buenos Aires to send delegates. The porteños expected an all-out attack momentarily, for Urquiza still had a sizable force. But no attack came.

Hoping that other provinces might be fearful of Urquiza, Mitre sent General Paz to explain why Buenos Aires feared his rule. The mission was a complete failure, for the provinces regarded Urquiza as the one who had ended the Rosas tyranny and the only hope of uniting the nation under one government. Most of the provinces were far more suspicious of Buenos Aires than of Urquiza. Buenos Aires was, after all, trying to retain for herself the customs duties that should have belonged to the whole nation.

Unlike many porteños, Mitre was genuinely interested in achieving national government. He had first to win the complete confidence of the province, and this was at least partly accomplished by his resistance to Urquiza. When a revolt broke out in Buenos Aires in favor of joining the Confederation, Mitre was the one who resisted it most effectively. Urquiza, to bring the bitter civil strife to an end, sent a delegation to try to make peace between the warring factions. Buenos Aires agreed to re-enter the Confederation if she could have deputies in proportion to her population. Urquiza, however, insisted on equal representation for all provinces regardless of population.

Buenos Aires drew up her own constitution. Mitre spoke in favor of a strong legislature to offset the power of the president. The constitution provided for the possibility of union with the Confederation, and Mitre wrote a number of newspaper articles in which he declared that Buenos Aires could not remain separated from the nation. Buenos Aires must be the center of the nation, for she was the region of liberalism, according to Mitre. The government must make an agreement with the Confederation by which union could be achieved in the future. In 1854 a treaty was signed with the Confederation; it provided for peace, common defense, and commerce, and agreed that both sides would work for reunion.

Almost by accident Mitre became interested in history. The historian Andrés Lamas wrote to him from Uruguay asking for copies of some documents about General Belgrano. Mitre began working in the archives, and became so interested in the independence struggles that he began writing articles on Belgrano. The result was that Mitre wrote a two-volume study, the *Historia de Belgrano y la independencia Argentina*. In 1856 he organized the Instituto Histórico-Geográfico del Río de la Plata. This was the kind of activity Mitre loved most, but he never refused to serve in the Army or in office when asked. He would soon be called on again, for a showdown between the province and the Confederation could not be postponed forever. The Confederation simply could not exist economically without Buenos Aires, which contained 90 per cent of the area's wealth. In 1857 Mitre became Minister of Government for Buenos Aires. He arranged for an exposition of native arts, and had other plans for cultural development. The financial plight of the Confederation led to increased pressure. Mitre declared in favor of free trade, saying Buenos Aires had a moral obligation to other provinces to allow them to move their commerce freely by land as well as by water. As the Confederation grew desperate, both sides prepared for war. Mitre was placed in charge of the army of Buenos Aires.

In October, 1859, the two armies met at Cepeda. Urquiza had an ill-armed force of about 14,000, while Mitre commanded around 8,000 men who were better equipped. Part of Mitre's force broke and fled with great loss of equipment. During the night Mitre withdrew his entire force to defend the city of Buenos Aires. He saved only 2,000 men. Although it was no clear-cut defeat, the porteños were alarmed and demoralized. Mitre quickly reorganized the defenses, and demanded that the Confederation's constitution be revised. Urquiza agreed to discuss the matter.

A new pact of union was signed, which met all porteño demands. Urquiza welcomed Buenos Aires back into the union, and declared a day of national thanksgiving. Not all porteños were satisfied, but Mitre tried to ensure their cooperation.

In February, 1860, Santiago Derqui was elected president of the Confederation, while Mitre was chosen as governor of Buenos Aires province. This election brought Mitre into national prominence. He worked to restore Buenos Aires' leadership of the nation. He and Urquiza exchanged friendly letters, and agreed that they both sought the same goal.

All was not peace and harmony for long. The Buenos Aires deputies were refused admission to the national congress, an act intended to irritate the sensitive porteños. Tempers soared, and Mitre and Urquiza fell out. The disagreement arose over the method of electing the deputies, and it should have been easily settled. Instead, no one was willing to make the first gesture toward conciliation. In the break-off of relations, Mitre and Urquiza both had some responsibility. Once more both sides prepared for war. It seems possible that Mitre may have realized that this was the time to place Buenos Aires at the head of the nation. The Confederation had no funds, and its troops lacked enthusiasm.

Urquiza waited at Pavón, where he felt the valley would aid in the defense of his inferior force. Mitre's infantry overpowered Urquiza's artillery. Seeing this loss, and abhorring needless bloodshed, Urquiza withdrew as Mitre had done at Cepeda. Urquiza retired to his ranch in Entre Ríos.

The victory at Pavón left Mitre the unrivaled leader of the nation, for President Derqui went into exile. Mitre's first problem was to hold back the porteños, who were eager to take revenge against the Confederation. The porteños were more difficult to control than the defeated Confederation, and it took great tact and talent on Mitre's part to heal the wounds. Urquiza wrote that Mitre was the one to reorganize the nation. It was no easy task, as Urquiza well knew.

In 1862 Mitre was the choice for president of the nation, the most popular man in the entire land. In organizing his government, he was careful to choose able and respected men. Ten years of waiting were now rewarded by an opportunity to create a genuine Argentine nation, and Mitre proceeded with wisdom and caution.

Mitre won over the provincial leaders, but met resistance in his home province. He refused to beat down the provinces and force them to accept porteño supremacy. It was no easy matter for him to complete what Urquiza had started without driving his porteño friends to rebellion. Mitre favored making Buenos Aires a federal district, for this was the only logical solution to the "Capital Question."

The porteños rejected this proposal, but agreed that Buenos Aires should serve as capital of the nation and the province for five years. The final solution had to be postponed, for forcing the issue at this time would have revived the bitterness and rivalries of the past. It was not until 1880 that Buenos Aires finally became the permanent federal district and national capital of Argentina.

In 1862 the customs house in Buenos Aires was nationalized, and its revenues now went to the nation rather than to the province. Argentina was also able to float a loan in England, and Mitre used the money to stimulate the economy. Commerce expanded rapidly even though the nation was involved in the bitter and costly war with Paraguay.

Underpopulation was another serious problem, for Argentina was an empty land. "To govern is to populate," said Alberdi, and Mitre agreed. He urged passage of a law calling for a national census, so the government would know its human resources. The census was begun before his term ended. To aid in the expansion of population and commerce, he encouraged the building of railroads and laying out of telegraph lines.

Education was another concern, and in this Mitre had powerful support from Domingo F. Sarmiento, who had studied the American teacher-training program of Horace Mann. The number of schools and of students enrolled increased rapidly in the next few years.

Mitre was also one of the founders of the famous newspaper *La Nación Argentina,* in 1862. Later, after his presidential term ended, he served as its editor. In the meantime he continued his studies of the independence era. His special interest, after Belgrano, was General José de San Martín, who had liberated Chile and led an expedition into Peru. San Martín's son-in-law, Mariano Balcarce, gave to Mitre San Martín's enormous collection of documents. Some of his countrymen demanded to know how he happened to have time to study history when his duties were so heavy. "In spite of the fact that the duties of government absorb almost all of my time," he replied, "I want to dedicate some hours of quiet to . . . the study of Argentine history."

Mitre's presidential term unfortunately coincided with the Paraguayan War, in which Argentina, Brazil, and Uruguay formed an alliance against Paraguay. The war was unpopular in Argentina, and there were riots in the provinces. The Indians on the southern frontier took advantage of the withdrawal of troops from the frontier military posts, and raided ranches and towns. It was a difficult time, yet Mitre's main concerns were making the national government function effectively and establishing a system of courts. He sent Dr. Manuel Rafael García to the United States to study the court system of a democracy.

During the Paraguayan War Mitre was commander in chief of the allied forces for two years, and left Vice President Marcos Paz in charge of the government. In January of 1868 the vice president died, and Mitre gave up his military post. The time for the presidential election was approaching. Unlike many other presidents, he refused to interfere or even to express a preference for any candidate, though he undoubtedly could have named his successor if he had wished. In October, 1868, Sarmiento succeeded to the presidency.

The Paraguayan War, which began in 1865, was still far from ended, despite the fact that Argentina, Brazil, and Uruguay were pitted against Paraguay. The allies expected the war to be brief, but the knowledge that Brazil and Argentina planned to divide Paraguay between them induced the Paraguayans to fight to the death in the most literal meaning of the term. When Mitre gave up field command of the allied forces, Argentina left the war largely to Brazil, and it was Brazilian troops who finally killed Francisco Solano López, the Paraguayan dictator.

When Mitre retired from the presidency he was still a poor man, for he had ignored all opportunities for financial gain, a policy too few Latin American officials have followed. A group of men in Buenos Aires, realizing his needy situation, gave him a house on Calle San Martín, where he lived the remainder of his life. He was forty-seven when his term ended, and his life was only a little more than half over. Though he served for a time as senator, his political career thenceforth was to be largely that of elder statesman.

In 1870 he became editor of the newspaper he had helped establish, and renamed it *La Nación*. It became one of the great papers of the continent. It remains today an important paper, still supporting democratic government as it did in his day.

In 1871 an epidemic of yellow fever struck Buenos Aires Province, and many people fled. The Mitres remained to help care for the ill. Mitre, his wife, Delfina, and their son Bartolito were all infected, but all recovered. The city bestowed a gold medal on the Mitres in gratitude for their service and sacrifice.

The following year President Sarmiento named Mitre envoy extraordinary to Brazil, to try to iron out grave difficulties arising out of the defeat of Paraguay. There was much talk of war between Argentina and Brazil, and feelings were high. On his arrival in Rio de Janeiro, Mitre was not given the customary courtesies granted to visiting diplomats. Had he returned in anger to Buenos Aires, war would have followed. Instead, he remained calm and patient, and after five months won the Brazilians over to a more compromising attitude. In the end he was as widely hailed in Brazil as in Argentina. Never had he been more popular.

Because there was much talk of Mitre succeeding Sarmiento as president, and because Sarmiento had decided to support Nicolás Avellaneda, Mitre was sent on another mission, this time to Asunción, Paraguay. He carried out his instructions, and reached agreement with the Paraguayan government. At that time he received new instructions from Sarmiento, to demand cession of regions to which Argentina had no claim. He asked Sarmiento to withdraw the demand, and on the president's refusal, resigned and returned to Buenos Aires. This time he found a cool reception; Sarmiento had ruined his chances for the presidency.

Mitre's friends insisted, nevertheless, that he allow his name to be used. He lost to Nicolás Avellaneda. His followers demanded a revolt; Mitre refused, stating that "the poorest of legal elections is better than the best of revolutions." He quickly left for Montevideo, to avoid being implicated in any revolt. But when his followers began a revolt, he felt obliged to return and assume the responsibility. Some of his critics maintained that he had planned the whole affair. If the charge was true, it seems that he had no intention of overthrowing the government, but wanted merely to issue a warning against manipulating elections.

After the revolt failed, Mitre was tried by court-martial. The majority voted for censure, loss of rank, and exile. Avellaneda revoked the sentence of exile, and eventually the rank was restored.

Mitre turned again to his study of history and his writing. His work on General San Martín grew to three volumes in length. In 1882 he traveled to Chile to visit the battlefield of Maipó, where San Martín and O'Higgins threw back a royalist invasion. In 1890 he went to Sevilla to study documents in the Archivo General de Indias. Many another disciple of Latin American history has followed his steps to Sevilla.

In 1890 Argentina was on the verge of financial collapse, largely because of the government's policies, which favored the big landowners at the expense of the nation. In Buenos Aires young men, many of them sons of immigrants, had formed the Radical Civic Union, which eventually became the Radical party that would later elect Hipólito Irigoyen as president of the nation. Mitre was in Europe when the Civic Union staged an ill-organized revolt. The rebels failed to capture the government, but President Juárez Celmán resigned. Mitre meanwhile visited Garibaldi's daughter in Italy, and in Paris saw Dom Pedro II of Brazil, who had been deposed the previous year.

The Radical Civic Union nominated Mitre for the presidency because of his great popularity and prestige as a liberal. Though he received enthusiastic support when he campaigned, he knew that the government controlled the electoral machinery and that it would not permit him to win.

The government offered to support Mitre if he dropped Bernardo Irigoyen, his Civic Union vice presidential running mate. Mitre accepted. He stated in *La Nación* that he did so to avoid an electoral struggle in which the Civic Union would surely have lost.

The Civic Union leaders felt that they had been tricked, and they split the party. Mitre tried to convince them that his was the only way of arranging honest elections in the future, but they refused to listen. Although he knew the government's support virtually guaranteed his election, Mitre withdrew his name.

In 1894 Mitre was elected to the senate once more. He served on the Commission for the Second Census, and he helped settle the boundary dispute with Chile. Although the disputed area had no apparent value, both nations had become aroused over it, and national pride demanded action. Mitre, who still had many friends in Chile, helped restore calm. In the end both sides agreed that war between Argentina and Chile was unthinkable.

The last notable public appearance that Mitre made was on his eightieth birthday, June 26, 1901. It was a national celebration, a legal holiday. The tremendous popularity and prestige he had earned were best expressed by President Julio A. Roca. While escorting a distinguished visitor through the streets of Buenos Aires, Roca pointed to Mitre's modest home. "There," he said, "lives a man who without a congress, an army, a fleet, or anything more than his name, is the strongest power existing in the Republic today."

This same house, the gift of grateful admirers many years before, Mitre willed to the nation along with the valuable library he had gathered. The Institución Mitre and the Academia Nacional de Historia both came to be located there after his death in 1906.

Mitre's lifelong devotion to democracy and liberty helped to establish them as part of Argentina's cultural tradition. Though democracy occasionally gives way to dictatorship, and liberty vanishes, neither is ever forgotten by Argentines. And when they remember democracy and freedom, they remember Bartolomé Mitre. Among Argentina's heroes, his position is secure.

Hipólito Irigoyen
1852–1933

Irigoyen was born in Balvanera on July 13, 1852. In that same year the Argentine tyrant Juan Manuel de Rosas was defeated and forced into exile. Irigoyen's maternal grandfather, Leandro Antonio Alem, was accused of having been a member of the *mazorca,* Rosas' dreaded police, and was executed. In his youth Irigoyen suffered for his grandfather's political affiliations.

Both Irigoyen and his uncle, Leandro N. Alem, were frequently reminded of the family's connection with Rosas, and their early years were made unhappy by such public hostility toward them. At the age of nine Irigoyen attended the Colegio San José for a year, and made an excellent record, though he was never accepted by his classmates. The following year he transferred to the Colegio de la América del Sud, where his uncle taught philosophy.

During the Paraguayan War, Alem earned fame on the battlefield. Soon after the war ended he received his law degree, and was ready to pursue a political career. Irigoyen, who tried to model himself after his uncle, was appointed police commissioner in Balvanera, where Alem was public defender. During this work with the police, Irigoyen developed maturity and learned much of politics and of human behavior. He became extremely popular with the people of the district, for he did not employ force or terror. On one occasion he hunted down a dangerous criminal and ordered him to appear at his office the next day. The man meekly complied, though Irigoyen was unarmed.

In 1874 Irigoyen began studying for a law degree, while Alem served in the legislature of Buenos Aires Province. Irigoyen did not complete his legal courses. Having no other employment, he became a political organizer for the new Partido Republicano. In 1877 he ran for the legislature of Buenos Aires Province. Unlike other candidates he made no speeches or public appearances. He disliked crowds intensely. When he learned that he had been elected, he refused to accept his post because he felt it had been gained by electoral fraud. After an investigation proved that his election had been fair, he took his seat in the legislature.

In the legislature Irigoyen proved himself an eloquent speaker, though his political ideas were not remarkable. On occasion he lectured his colleagues on their absences or on their failure to follow the rules for addressing the chamber.

In 1880, when General Julio A. Roca was elected president,

Irigoyen was elected to the national legislature. In 1881 he was appointed to the Educational Control Committee, and abandoned forever his role in the legislature. He supported himself as a teacher of history, civics, and philosophy in the Escuela Normal de Maestros, or teachers' college. His wants were simple, for he cared little for money or for the material comforts it could provide.

In 1882 the city of Buenos Aires became the permanent Federal District, and the nation's most urgent political problem was solved. Thereafter Argentina was beyond danger of breaking up, and large numbers of European immigrants flowed into the country. Since it was difficult for the newcomers to acquire land, most of them went into commerce or some related activity in Buenos Aires. These people were badly hurt by the government's financial policies, for these favored the *estancieros,* the owners of huge estates. The *estancieros* were happy to have constant inflation, for they sold their wheat and beef abroad for stable currencies. With inflation of the Argentine peso, these men found their wealth growing. The rest of the country, and especially the merchants, suffered increasingly as the peso grew worthless and the national debt mounted. Because the government was the instrument of the *estancieros,* the plight of the merchants was ignored. The merchants and professional men began seeking political rather than economic solutions to their problems.

Young intellectuals gathered in Buenos Aires coffeehouses and discussed the country's worsening economic condition. Gradually an organized opposition to the government arose. In September, 1889, the young men of Buenos Aires called for a public demonstration of solidarity against the government and its policies. The role of immigrants and their sons in this movement was a prominent one. Their main demand was for the right to vote in honest elections. Leandro Alem was one of the principal leaders of this group. Its political activities increased rapidly, for the country's economy was approaching disaster.

Irigoyen took no part in these events, though the new party's ideals were similar to his own. The Unión Cívica, or Civic Union, attracted more and more supporters. Leandro Alem became the most popular member, and was elected president of the new party. Former President Bartolomé Mitre, an immensely popular figure still, was chosen to be the Civic Union's standard-bearer in case of successful revolution. Mitre opposed violence, though Alem and other leaders were sure that only by revolution could they wrest power from the landed oligarchs. A revolt was planned.

To attract Irigoyen to the Civic Union, he was offered the position of chief of the revolutionary police. Irigoyen at first refused, then accepted. The differences of opinion among groups and leaders made the projected revolt appear unpromising, and Mitre quietly left for Europe. In the end Alem was acknowledged as the proper one to head the government if the revolt succeeded.

The government began arresting leaders, and the rebels were forced to act hastily. Irigoyen opposed the revolt until more regiments were won over to the cause, to avoid unnecessary bloodshed. If most of the Army joined the rebels, the opposition would collapse. The revolt began in the early hours of July 26, 1890, even though too few regiments had been won over, and from the first things went badly for the rebels. By July 28th the revolt was over. Though the rebels failed to capture the government, President Juárez Celmán resigned, but his party remained in power.

The Civic Union decided to try to win the presidency with Mitre as its candidate. Mitre began negotiating an agreement with the Conservative party, and was denounced by Alem and Irigoyen. He called these leaders radicals. In July, 1891, they changed the party's title to that of Unión Cívica Radical, or Radical Civic Union. It was after this that Irigoyen began taking an active part.

The government tried to persuade all parties to agree on a candidate. Irigoyen insisted that the president be chosen by popular vote. When he was reminded of the revolution of 1890, he declared: "Comply with the laws and . . . you will not have to face any revolutions." His stand won him widespread respect. When one man called him a "petulant juvenile," Bartolomé Mitre came to his defense. "No, he is not petulant," he said, "but rather the hope of the country."

Aroused by the growing sentiment in favor of the U.C.R., the government declared a state of siege and arrested Alem. The election was then held as scheduled, and the government's candidate was declared the winner. This was Luis Sáenz Peña, who was determined to restore democratic principles. His own supporters opposed this, and blocked him at every turn. Once more the U.C.R. made plans for a revolution. In the meantime Irigoyen was quietly winning an unbreakable control over the U.C.R. supporters in Buenos Aires Province. Alem was much less successful in organizing and directing the party on the national level.

On July 30, 1893, the second U.C.R. revolution began. Irigoyen and his lieutenants seized the interior of Buenos Aires Province, and for a few days success seemed in sight. The situation changed quickly, and the city of Buenos Aires remained under the control of the government. Irigoyen shrugged off the defeat and continued building up his power.

Gradually all the U.C.R. leaders who were ahead of Irigoyen were eliminated. In 1890 Aristóbulo del Valle died. Juan B. Justo had already left the party to organize a socialist movement. In 1897 Lisandro de la Torre, who frequently accused Irigoyen of being greedy for power, abandoned the party.

Leandro Alem, bitter at his repeated failures, took his own life, leaving the leadership open to Irigoyen. Immediately after this, Irigoyen resumed his unusual habit of keeping out of public activities. He avoided large meetings, but sent countless manifestoes to his followers, urging them to remain faithful to the cause of effective suffrage.

Suffrage, effective suffrage, was Irigoyen's only goal. In the 1880's and 1890's this would have satisfied most liberals. In the twentieth century, however, laws to protect labor were demanded. Irigoyen never advanced beyond the goal of effective suffrage. He was to achieve this goal, but the triumph would prove hollow, for by that time other men were more interested in social legislation. To Irigoyen, the universal right to vote remained an end in itself rather than a means of changing society. He assumed that if everyone could vote, the proper changes would follow.

In the elections of 1910 the Radical party, as the Civic Union was now called, showed surprising strength in the interior provinces. The party came close to victory in Córdoba and won in Salta. The Salta victory was too shocking to the Conservatives to let stand; the election was annulled, and the Radicals boycotted the new one.

Roque Sáenz Peña, son of the former president, was elected in 1910. He sincerely desired honest elections for Argentina, and promised a sweeping reform. After the election he met secretly with Irigoyen to work out the new law. Impressed with Irigoyen's idealism and honesty, Sáenz Peña offered him a cabinet post from which to supervise elections. Irigoyen refused to serve the Conservative government.

The Sáenz Peña Law of 1912 coupled voting with registration for military service. The Radicals and Socialists prepared for the April, 1912, elections. The Radicals won a majority in the legislature of the federal capital and in Santa Fe Province. Thereafter the Radicals and Conservatives concentrated on preparing for the presidential election of 1916. The Radicals, by an overwhelming majority, nominated Irigoyen.

When a messenger went to inform Irigoyen, he was obliged to return with Irigoyen's refusal. Another messenger brought the explanation that Irigoyen wanted only to awaken the public need for a free vote. A delegation of party officials called on Irigoyen and informed him that the party would disband unless he agreed to be its candidate. Irigoyen accepted. He was elected by a narrow margin, 152 of 300 votes. This narrow margin he owed to Lisandro de la Torre, who considered him simply the lesser of two evils, and supported him.

Irigoyen's cabinet astonished Conservatives and Radicals alike, for it was composed of men known only for their faithfulness to the cause of free elections. To Irigoyen this was qualification enough. He apparently was unconcerned over the lack of knowledge of their ministerial fields. The Minister of Education had the mentality of a rural first-grade teacher, and the Minister of War was a "kind civilian" who knew nothing of military matters.

On his inauguration, however, Irigoyen was greeted by a spontaneous and delirious demonstration rarely equaled in Argentina. The crowd unhitched the horses from his carriage and drew it through the streets to the Casa Rosada (Pink House). Throughout this wild demonstration Irigoyen sat impassive and unsmiling.

Irigoyen was the first "man of the people" ever elected in Argentina, and extravagant hopes were held for his rule. Yet the Conservative oligarchy controlled the press, the educational system, the Congress, and the economy. The Conservative majority in the Senate was five to one. It was smaller in the Chamber, but was sufficient to block any proposed laws.

Since the Radicals had no real program Irigoyen spent the first months in office consolidating and expanding his personal sway. He visited government offices, reprimanding employees for their untidy appearances, and spent much time redrafting official letters to give them greater dignity. These actions did nothing to improve the nation in any concrete way, yet none of Irigoyen's devoted followers questioned his leadership.

The president of Argentina was given broad powers of appointment of officials, and Irigoyen exercised this right to an astonishing degree. He was, in fact, the chief personnel officer of the administration. Because he was reluctant to dismiss appointees of previous presidents, he simply created additional positions. His office became the rendezvous of the unemployed.

Irigoyen seems to have had only a vague and unclear view of the country's economic ills. His solutions were more government jobs and a hotly resisted attempt to reduce the popularity of gambling on horse races. He lived a simple life, and he believed that his countrymen could be persuaded to resist temptation with equal fortitude. This faith was largely misplaced.

The lower classes idolized Irigoyen, and expected miracles from him. They expected economic reform, but he did not look beyond giving them the right to a vote that counted. His view of the proper role of government was a means for funneling the desires of the various classes and arriving at reasonable solutions through democratic processes. He felt that the government must remain above partisanship in such matters. Unsure of Irigoyen's feelings, labor was reluctant to strike. Ultimately the government's passive role in labor disputes set off a chain reaction. The number of strikes grew enormously after the first year of his administration. The number of unions and of men involved in strikes grew even more rapidly. Irigoyen refused to intervene in strikes unless there was violence, and violence to him was injury to human beings, not property. "What is important," he said, "is the salvation of every human life."

The tension between labor and management mounted toward the danger point, yet Irigoyen expressed the belief that all was well and that class antagonism was disappearing. On January 7, 1919, however, the Semana Trágica (Tragic Week) began. It started with a strike at the Pedro Vasena e Hijos metalworks.

When the strike began, strikebreakers dispersed the crowd with bullets, and a number of strikers were killed. A mass funeral was held, and it was also broken up by gunfire and more killings. Labor unions responded with a general strike in Buenos Aires, and mobs roamed the streets. Their wrath was vented on business establishments, especially those that were owned by foreigners.

Mob rule lasted for five terrifying days. No one knows how many people were killed or the extent of the destruction. For six days Irigoyen refused to act, insisting that labor had no basis of complaint against the government. On the seventh day, however, he called out the troops. At this time the unions ordered the men back to work, and peace was quickly restored. All parties proclaimed their innocence, and all blamed Irigoyen's policy of nonintervention. For the remaining years of his first six-year term, Irigoyen paid careful attention to the needs of labor, but he was able to accomplish little. Thirty-three laws proposed by the administration were voted down. The greatest single defeat was the failure of the Labor Code in 1921. By this time the Radicals had a substantial majority in the Chamber, but were badly split between those who idolized Irigoyen and those who resented his personal rule.

Though Irigoyen's labor policies were not successful, his University Reform of 1918 has been hailed as an intelligent action. The universities had long been subject to intervention and open only to students from wealthy families. The reform was precipitated by demands from students at the University of Córdova. Students were appointed to advisory posts that enabled them to supervise the Universidad de Litoral. The reforms gave universities autonomy similar to that which they enjoyed in the Middle Ages, and made the students heard in university administration. The University Reform demonstrated that Irigoyen was capable of direct action when he perceived that there was danger.

Another aspect of Irigoyen's rule was his exercise of the president's power to intervene in the provinces. This constitutional power had been intended for the benefit of Conservative presidents faced with provincial opposition. Irigoyen, however, employed the power more widely than any of his Conservative predecessors. He intervened when elections were disputed. His enemies declared that Radical party control was his real goal. But unlike most of the presidents who had intervened in provincial elections earlier, when the vote of supervised elections proved unfavorable Irigoyen accepted it. Honest elections remained his highest goal, though the country still demanded other reforms of a socioeconomic nature.

World War I began two years before Irogoyen assumed the presidency. He did not officially declare a policy, but he kept Argentina neutral. Argentina split into two groups, neutral and pro-Ally. The former, among whom were pro-German elements, hoped to reap great profits by sales to both sides. Irigoyen was pushed by neutral and pro-Ally partisans, but he ignored all views except his own. He retained this attitude even when it was learned that the German Ambassador to Argentina had asked the German government that two Argentine ships be spared "or else sunk without a trace being left." Irigoyen grimly maintained neutrality even though most of his countrymen wished to support the Allies, and were outraged at the inhumane suggestion.

The instructions Irigoyen gave the Argentine delegation to Europe after the war indicated that he still clung to simple, humanitarian values. Their instructions were to insist that all countries be admitted to the League as equals. In any discussion of the war no distinction was to be made between victor or vanquished, belligerent or neutral. The Argentine delegation was also to stand firmly against any nation expanding its territory by force.

The constitution prevented the president from being immediately re-elected. In 1922 Marcelo T. Alvear was elected as the Radical party's successor to Irigoyen. The party split into two wings—those who remained devoted to Irigoyen and those who supported Alvear. In 1928, despite this split, Irigoyen moved into the Casa Rosada for his second term as president.

The second term was a complete fiasco. Irigoyen was in his eighties, and unable to comprehend the severe economic crisis that paralyzed Argentina when the Great Depression began. Effective leadership was needed more than ever, but Irigoyen had grown too feeble to provide it. It was said that he would sign any paper placed before him. Some of his associates used the opportunity to enrich themselves through fraud and graft.

As the financial crisis heightened, Argentina was on the verge of revolution. On September 5, 1930, Dr. Alfredo L. Palacios, Dean of the Buenos Aires Law School, called on Irigoyen and asked him to resign for the good of the country. Astonished and bewildered, Irigoyen complied.

It was too late to save the country. Early next morning the people of Buenos Aires were awakened by low-flying fighter and bomber planes. Soon troops marched through the streets, with General José Félix Uriburu at their head. Mobs looted buildings where Radical party politicians frequently gathered. They surged into Irigoyen's cheap apartment and threw his iron cot into the street.

The Radical party's efforts ended in failure. Irigoyen, Argentina's first popularly elected president, expected that through honest and democratic elections all problems would be solved. The party's failure was a tragedy for Argentina, for a harsh military dictatorship was imposed on the country for the next quarter of a century. Even more than thirty years after the downfall of Irigoyen, the Radical party has not recovered from the disaster. The man who sought effective suffrage and honest elections "buried democracy in Argentina," according to Lisandro de la Torre. The Argentinians, disillusioned by the failure of the man they had chosen, turned increasingly to the Army.

María Eva Duarte de Perón
1919–1952

Although her life was short, "Evita" Perón will long be remembered, for a variety of reasons. She was born on May 7, 1919, in Toldos, Argentina, a small town in Buenos Aires Province. Her mother was Juana Ibarguen. Her father was Juan Duarte. Her parents were not married; her father was legally married to another, and lived with his legal family. Evita lived with her mother, three sisters, and one brother.

The amount of schooling she had is difficult to determine, for the accounts vary from only the primary grades to two years of high school. Her father died when she was very young, perhaps two years old.

After the father's death the family moved to Junín, not far from Toldos. There the mother ran a boardinghouse. Some time after her schooling ended, Evita moved to Buenos Aires. She worked for Radio Belgrano as an actress, though she apparently had no dramatic training. Her salary was a modest 150 pesos a month. Friends who knew her when she was a second-rate radio actress remember that she used to say: "I *will* be somebody. I can just feel it. I will be somebody someday." She was right. During this time she became acquainted with General Ramírez, who rose to power after the Army revolt of 1943. She learned quickly how to take advantage of official influence, and her salary soared to 5,000 pesos a month. By 1945 this same job paid her 35,000 pesos a month. According to a legend, she called General Ramírez on the telephone, and her voice charmed him into meeting her.

As her salary rose, Evita began wearing expensive clothes. She was five feet five inches tall, but her "upsweep" hairdo made her appear taller. Her eyes were dark brown. Her hair was blonde with a reddish tint, and her skin was white. She was attractive, and she enhanced her natural beauty with beauty aids and with stylish clothes. She was, according to accounts, "equally impressive in a strapless evening gown, a two-piece light print, or floppy slacks."

It is not known with certainty when Evita and Juan Domingo Perón met. One story is that after a disastrous earthquake in San Juan, Perón put on a fund-raising campaign for relief of the disaster area. One of those seated on the stage was radio actress Evita Perón. Seated next to Perón was a tango singer, Libertad la Marque, who had donated her services. When she arose to perform, Evita, according to the legend, took her place beside Perón. By leading the applause wildly, Evita kept the singer giving encores until she and Perón had become acquainted.

However they met, they made a remarkable political team. There are many who maintain that Evita was the more astute of the two. Whether or not this was true, Perón's decline was rapid after her death in 1952. The 1943 Army coup gave Perón an opportunity to begin political manipulations. At first he operated behind the scenes; then he gradually emerged as the spokesman for the G.O.U. (United Officer Group), which was conspiring to dominate the Army and through it the nation. The G.O.U. was composed of young, highly nationalistic officers. There were other groups seeking power, but they were confused as to their goals. The G.O.U. knew what it wanted—an Argentina patterned after the régimes of Mussolini and Hitler. Perón had spent some years in Europe, particularly in Italy and Germany. The "Leader principle" appealed to him.

While Perón was head of the Ministry of Labor, Evita organized radio artists and workers into an industry-wide union. She was thus able to put all radio stations to work in an enormous propaganda campaign to present Perón as a Latin superman. In mid-1945 opposition to her tactics became so strong that she was forced out of her job temporarily, but she was soon back.

In October of 1945 Perón's opponents in the Army and Navy became fearful and envious of his meteoric rise toward political power. Together they forced him to resign from his government posts as head of the ministries of Labor and War, and as vice president. He went into hiding, but was soon found and arrested.

Within an hour after Perón's fall from power, Evita was fired by officials of Radio Belgrano, who were no doubt tired of her domineering ways. Their action was premature and unwise. Evita never forgot a slight, and this was a major insult. She kept a hate list, and she waited for a chance for revenge against those whose names were on it. Her hatreds included groups such as Argentina's political and social "oligarchy," which had scorned her, nations such as the United States, and a multitude of unfortunate individuals, such as the officials of Radio Belgrano.

Perón was imprisoned on Martín García island. Evita called together leaders of the *descamisados* (shirtless ones, or workingmen) and labor unions, and outlined the strategy for them to follow. *Descamisados* flocked into Buenos Aires from all directions, and a tremendous mob assembled before the Government House, where Perón's foes were trying to organize their own administration.

Meanwhile Perón had pretended serious illness, and had been brought, under guard, to a hospital in Buenos Aires. As the mob grew larger and more violent the government officials became fearful, and hesitated to use force. The crowd kept shouting Perón's name and demanding to see him. Finally the government gave in and permitted him to appear on the balcony. He was given a tumultuous greeting. On October 17th he was released, and he returned to power much stronger than before. Evita's skillful use of the *descamisados* not only saved him from oblivion but also launched him toward the presidency. A few days after his release, he and Evita were married.

Perón did not take up his former posts. He placed trusted friends in these and other key positions, while he concentrated on his campaign for the elections of February, 1946. His supporters organized the Labor party, which nominated him for the presidency. Evita, now his close political adviser, campaigned by his side, something no presidential candidate's wife had ever done. Together they made a striking team, both physically attractive, both excellent speakers and crowd-pleasers. Perón won handily.

In this election, and in many other triumphs, Perón owed a large part of his success to the absolute devotion of his extraordinary wife. After he took office she moved into the Ministry of Labor and Social Welfare, his former center of power, and for practical purposes she was the Secretary of Labor. She gained control of the General Confederation of Labor, and placed her friends in key positions in various unions. Her influence and authority were used for the purpose of aiding Perón, but at the same time she was the driving force in the program to aid the poor. She never forgot her own humble beginnings, and among her many motivations she seems to have had a sincere desire to help the downtrodden.

Evita worked ceaselessly to solidify the affections and loyalty of the *descamisados*. She toured factories, housing developments, and workers' districts. Her methods were ever unorthodox but successful. On these tours she dressed in her finest furs and jewels, in her Parisian clothes. The *descamisados* loved her for it; to them she was a beautiful symbol of a working girl who had made good. Although Evita made little headway in winning over the upper and middle classes, she was quite successful in charming the diplomatic corps by attentions and favors.

As president, Perón announced a Five-Year Plan for Argentine development. It was a catalogue of proposed reforms and plans for economic and social development. At Evita's suggestion one of these reforms was women's suffrage. When it was approved, she founded the Peronista Women's party, which gave him loyal and enthusiastic support. It is no surprise, with Evita as their leader, that they demanded the re-election of Perón in 1952. In 1949 he had the Constitution changed to permit a second term. Other worthwhile and needed changes made it possible for the poor to attend the universities. At the same time, however, Perón tightened his control over the universities, to make them, like labor unions, a presidential instrument.

Partly at Evita's urging, a great number of social-welfare projects were launched. She supervised the new Ministry of Health, and encouraged the building of hospitals and clinics, and campaigns to eradicate diseases. Some of these campaigns, such as the elimination of malaria, were completely successful and widely beneficial.

Evita also founded the Social Aid (Eva Perón) Foundation. There had been a similar institution in Buenos Aires since the 1820's, the domain of the ladies of Argentina's high society. Since these ladies snubbed Evita, she founded her own welfare establishment. It was financed by huge gifts from labor unions and industrialists, in response to her "forceful appeals." It must have been painful, indeed, to the industrialists to make such donations, but they knew too well the dangers of refusing.

Both of the Peróns were unorthodox in their behavior. While some people were shocked, many were pleased. At the presidential inaugural banquet, for example, Evita appeared in an evening gown that left one shoulder bare. Tradition called for the First Lady to dress more conventionally and with much less exposure. Evita and her gown caused a sensation. Photographs showed her happily at ease; but the archbishop who sat next to her exposed shoulder apparently kept his eyes on his plate. Argentines had never seen anyone like her before.

No woman, except perhaps Doña Encarnación, wife of the nineteenth-century dictator, Rosas, had ever been so influential or taken such an active part in Argentine affairs before. Evita was often compared to Doña Encarnación and, curiously, to the late Eleanor Roosevelt, but the similarities to the latter were superficial. Evita called cabinet ministers as well as union leaders to her office, and they had no choice but to comply. When she was displeased with them, they were in for tongue-lashings. Small wonder the rumor began to spread that Perón was really a henpecked husband.

In 1947, when everything was going his way, Perón dreamed of making Argentina the leader not only of Latin America but of the whole Latin world. Evita made a triumphal tour of Spain, Italy, and France. In Rome she received a decoration from the Pope. Francisco Franco of Spain gave her the order of Isabel la Católica, and she was similarly honored in France, though the country had not recovered from World War II. One French commentator ungenerously remarked that "Madame Perón will be made palatable to the French workers and peasants by being dressed as a piece of Argentine frozen beef." Although Evita was well received everywhere, nothing came of Perón's grandiose dream except a few commercial treaties.

Evita proved to be an invaluable political ally for Perón, and her popularity with the *descamisados* was extraordinary. They literally worshiped her. To them she was a beautiful Lady Bountiful who knew their needs and spoke their language and who also secured a multitude of tangible benefits for them. She could harangue huge crowds as effectively and movingly as any union organizer.

Her devotion to Perón was passionate and complete, and it never wavered. In many speeches she compared him to the Argentine independence hero General José de San Martén, to San Martín's disadvantage. The Congress was not to be outdone in fawning gestures. In the spring of 1952 it named him "Liberator of the Republic," without indicating from what or whom or when this feat was achieved. At the same time Evita was named "Spiritual Chief of the Nation." She was, in fact, the spiritual inspiration of the *descamisados*.

One vital reason for the early brilliant success of Perón's presidential career was that Evita took over the enormous task of keeping the *descamisados* loyal and contented. Perón had first thought of rousing up this group to political activity, but when Evita took over his work with the *descamisados,* it aided him greatly. In the first place it enabled him to concentrate on the traditional arbiter of politics in Argentina, the military. By no longer making the rounds of *descamisado* projects, he no longer found it advisable to remove his shirt and pretend to work while photographers captured flattering views of his muscular physique. As a campaigner, these photos did no harm, especially after women were given the right to vote. But as president it was more appropriate to divide the labors with Evita, and to maintain his role of officer and gentleman. The Army did not look favorably on his stirring up the *descamisados*.

Evita's hold over the *descamisados* also helped Perón maintain a delicate balance between the two major clusters of power, labor and the military. Although Perón has been called a dictator, he always had to struggle and remain alert to stay in power. The balancing act required artistry and skill, and for a time this remarkable team displayed a fine touch. Evita's share in laying down major policies and in making major decisions probably will never be known. One may be sure, however, that she held firm opinions on every matter and that she expressed these views forcibly and perhaps repeatedly.

The Social Aid Foundation, with its ample funds for which no accounting was necessary, was both a genuine welfare organization and a propaganda device. In addition to its emergency activities, disease eradication programs, and hospitals, it ran food and clothing stores in which everything was sold at low prices. The use of the welfare foundation for propaganda was distasteful to many people, and it obscured the fact that the foundation pursued serious activities. On one occasion Evita sent a large shipment of clothing for needy children in Washington. This gesture of Argentina helping the United States must have given great satisfaction to many Latin Americans. Since the United States enjoyed a uniquely high position on Evita's hate list, the act was obviously meant to embarrass the "Colossus of the North." It succeeded.

In 1951, for a short time, it appeared that Evita might become Argentina's first lady vice president. There were several reasons other than her illness and death in 1952 for her failure to achieve the vice presidency. She and Perón staged a tremendous rally for the occasion. The *descamisados* were expected to turn out in force—at least one million, so that the Army and the nation would be awed into accepting her as Perón's running mate. For once, however, the *descamisados* did not respond to her summons. Only a quarter of the number expected appeared. At the same time the Army high command informed Perón that it would not accept a woman vice president. Supposing something happened to Perón? The Army would be under a woman commander in chief. Unthinkable!

In August, 1951, Evita tearfully withdrew her name. This was a decision, she said, that "I have taken by myself." By lopping a few years off her age, she could show that she was too young to serve as constitutional vice president. Tension between Perón and the Army remained, and in September there was an abortive revolt. It failed mainly because the rebels could not agree among themselves, and also because Perón's campaign to win the loyalty of soldiers and noncommissioned officers had succeeded. Some regiments simply disobeyed orders, and refused to join the revolt.

In November, Evita underwent an operation, and it was rumored that she was seriously ill, dying of cancer. A semiautobiographical book, *The Meaning of My Life*, was hastily written. There was in it actually very little about her life. Its purpose was simply to make sure that after death the *descamisados* would remain loyal to Perón. This book was made a required text in schools of all levels, including the university.

Evita's book, which she did not write herself, almost caused an international incident. Publishers in the United States refused to publish an English translation of it, though they would have been delighted to publish a genuine autobiography of Evita. Argentines, who were accustomed to the government making decisions in such cases, would not believe that the publishers arrived at this decision by themselves. They charged the American State Department with censorship, and the United States Information Service building in Buenos Aires was bombed twice, in June and July of 1952.

On her last public appearance, on May Day, 1952, Evita showed that her loyalty and devotion to Perón were undiminished. She made a brief but fiery speech. "My dear *descamisados*," she said, "the enemy is preparing an ambush for us. Stand by Perón, who stands by you. . . ."

On July 26, 1952, Evita died of cancer at the age of thirty-three. Argentina was plunged into a week of massive mourning the like of which has seldom been seen anywhere in the world. The *descamisados*, as might be expected, were the chief mourners, for they had lost their ideal and champion. They demanded that she be canonized as "Saint Eva of America."

Evita's body, like that of Lenin, was to be permanently on view, and for this purpose a glass-topped coffin was ordered from the United States. A special building was erected for this memorial. The architect was a Peronista in good standing, and the building was higher than the Statue of Liberty. The *descamisados* noted these facts, and knew that Evita would have been pleased.

After her death a power struggle took place as Perón moved to prevent the survival of an organized following devoted to Evita rather than to himself. He took over her most important duties, such as running the Social Aid Foundation and the Peronista Women's party.

Juan Duarte, Evita's brother, had served as Perón's secretary, and had grown rich in the process. He was found dead of a gunshot wound in the head, a revolver in his hand, and a suicide note nearby. The press made much of the suicide angle, but Argentines remained unconvinced. "We know he committed suicide," they said. "But we don't know who helped him."

Without his able partner, Perón bungled from one crisis to another. He deserted the *descamisados* and courted the industrialists. He antagonized the landowners and alienated the Church and the Army. In 1955, just three years after Evita's death, he was driven out of the country. Although Peronistas remained a powerful force ten years later, the Army still wanted no more of Perón.

PART VII

Three Political Innovators

Two of these men served as president of their country. All of them left lasting marks on their societies, though their influence has not always been fortunate or desirable.

When Guzmán Blanco became president of Venezuela, the troubled land badly needed a leader of his ability. "Venezuela is a barracks," said Simón Bolívar after liberating his native land from Spanish rule. And so it has remained, almost to the present. Venezuela's first civilian president to complete his term of office was Rómulo Betancourt (1959–1964). Guzmán Blanco could have made Venezuelan political life something more worth while than a greedy scramble for spoils by Army officers. Instead, he introduced a system for acquiring vast wealth through political office that has been followed by Venezuelan presidents down to the time of Betancourt. If Venezuela could recover the funds stolen by her politicians in the past century, she probably could afford to lend money to her neighbors.

González Prada was a Peruvian, and during his time Peru was badly governed. Although Peru had been one of the two most important viceroyalties in the colonial era, as an independent nation she could not achieve effective and stable government. As in Mexico, the wealthy and educated were indifferent to the needs of the country. González Prada attacked the various evils, and aroused the national conscience. His biting comments were not welcome, and he was accused of being a malcontent and an atheistic troublemaker, but his ideas could not be ignored. Peru is still far from solving all her political and economic problems, but the fact that she has made a beginning was largely owing to the ceaseless efforts of González Prada.

Uruguay's start as an independent nation was also most unpromising, for her population was small, her resources few, and her civil strife endless. Batlle's program was to end the civil wars by removing the causes of them, and in this he succeeded. He also introduced the idea of government participation in economic affairs and government responsibility for public well-being. By adopting Batlle's program, Uruguay has enjoyed a respite from civil conflict and a vast extension of government benefits. The government, however, has more often simply yielded to public demands than it has taken the lead in economic development. As a result the government is paying out so much more than it receives that it seems to be heading for bankruptcy.

Antonio Guzmán Blanco
1830–1899

Guzmán Blanco was born in Caracas in 1830, the same year that Venezuela adopted a constitution designed to reduce the political turbulence that was already becoming characteristic. This constitution limited voting and officeholding to persons of property. Other clauses also favored persons of wealth. These provisions were an expression of the fear of liberty and change in a land where violence was common.

Guzmán Blanco's father was a Liberal politician who was sentenced to death for political activity. Guzmán Blanco and his mother went to President José Tadeo Monagas to plead for the

Antônio Guzmán Blanco (1830-1899)
Reorganizer of Venezuela and creator of
unfortunate traditions.

Manuel González Prada (1848-1918)
Intellectual leader of Peruvian youth and
the conscience of Peru.

José Batlle y Ordónez (1865-1929)
The creator of modern Uruguay, the
multiple-executive, and the welfare
state.

Joaquim Nabuco de Araujo (1849-1910) Lawyer, scholar, statesman, and abolitionist of Brazil.

Getulio D. Vargas (1883-1954) Dictator and modernizer of Brazil, and founder of the New State.

father's life. The president heeded their plea, and the family went into exile.

In 1844 the Conservative oligarchy attacked Monagas because of his leniency toward his Liberal opponents. The Liberals came to his support, and he switched sides. The Liberals were now in power, and they abolished the death penalty for political crimes, to protect themselves in the future.

Guzmán Blanco went through the courses of the academy of Montenegro, then studied medicine and law. He was convinced, however, that politics offered the only sure hope of winning wealth and prestige. His father became vice president under Monagas, and Guzmán Blanco was sent on a diplomatic mission to the Venezuelan consulate in New York and then to the embassy in Washington. He returned to join the new Liberal leader, Juan C. Falcón, in the Federal War, a bitter war between the Liberals and the Conservatives.

In 1859 Falcón was driven into exile, and Guzmán Blanco accompanied him. This was a turning point in his career, for Falcón came to depend on him so much that he rose to second place among Liberal leaders.

When they returned to Venezuela, Guzmán Blanco began publishing a newspaper, the *Eco del Ejército* (Echo of the Army). He constantly praised Falcón, and at the same time made his own name better known. Guzmán Blanco's career is an excellent example of an intelligent and ambitious man carefully and patiently plotting his rise to power. He realized that military rank and experience were necessary to achieve his goal. He procured a post in the Army, and displayed superb skill and strategy in battle. After he defeated the Conservative forces at Salina Cruz, he was promoted, and the way was open for him to become a general. Falcón disliked dealing with the military chiefs, and he left this task to Guzmán Blanco. As a result Guzmán Blanco was able to win the loyalty of the officers, a loyalty that would aid him greatly in the future.

The Federal War had gone on four years, and had caused great destruction and waste. Guzmán Blanco entered into negotiations with the Conservative leaders, and was instrumental in ending the war. This was a master stroke that made his countrymen recognize him as a man of reason, firmness, peace, and patriotism. Some of his critics claimed that it was mere opportunism and that he gained considerable money in the bargain.

The country was ruined by the Federal War, which followed half a century of barracks revolts. Guzmán Blanco was to play an important part in reconstruction. He was anxious to create a stable political system, improve transportation and commerce, and extend the schools to make education available. He was also determined to force the Church to give up its political activities. While doing these things, Guzmán Blanco gave himself "commissions" that also fattened his own bank accounts at home and abroad, so that he became wealthy.

When Falcón became provisional president, Guzmán Blanco became vice president and the real chief executive. His power was delegated to him by Falcón, and his position depended on the president's favor. Most of the time Falcón preferred to live away from the capital, leaving administration of the country to Guzmán Blanco.

The tasks on which Guzmán Blanco concentrated at first were foreign loans, constitutional reforms, and that of proving to the country that he should be president in his own right. In 1863 he sailed to Europe as both Vice President and Minister of the Treasury and of Foreign Relations. His purpose was to negotiate a loan to reimburse and reward the Liberals for the cost of the Federal War.

He negotiated a loan of half a million pounds, then hurried home to obtain legislative approval of it. Though there was opposition to the loan, Guzmán Blanco triumphed, and a substantial part of the loan was his personal reward. During the next four years he obtained other loans for Venezuela, reserving part of them for himself, and his wealth was established.

At the same time Guzmán Blanco worked at pacifying the country and winning the support of the provincial *caudillos*. He reorganized the national finances, and endeared himself to the Army by seeing to it that it was paid regularly. He pushed railroad construction and road building, for Venezuela was woefully deficient in means of transportation.

Guzmán Blanco's opponents worked to undermine Falcón's confidence in him, because they feared him far more than Falcón. By constantly reminding Falcón of Guzmán Blanco's ambitions, they won their objective.

Falcón realized that Guzmán Blanco had grown too powerful for him to make an open break. He sent Guzmán Blanco on another mission to Europe, where he had the opportunity of arranging other profitable loans. Falcón returned to Caracas, but delegated official duties to two men who were enemies of Guzmán Blanco.

This plot did not work, for there was soon a rebellion that caused Falcón to leave the country. From Paris, Guzmán Blanco watched and waited. When the time came, he returned to take over as Liberal leader. From the island of Curaçao he prepared for war. The local *caudillos*, whose loyalty he had won earlier, supported him, and their support was decisive. In 1870 Guzmán Blanco landed on the coast, and marched to Caracas.

While fighting continued sporadically in different parts of the country, Guzmán Blanco prepared to take over as absolute dictator. He turned against his opponents with vengeance. Students in the universities demonstrated against him. He interfered with the universities, to punish the students, not to improve their education. Students who opposed him were expelled, and some classes were suspended.

To help the country recover, Guzmán Blanco abolished export duties and reduced those on imports by 70 per cent. He reorganized the tax system, which had not been changed since 1830. He also decreed that the government assume the debts of peons who had supported him in his struggle for power.

Guzmán Blanco at this time was forty-one years old, at the height of his physical power. He possessed what no rival had:

real ability in political and administrative affairs. He had finally worked his way up to the pinnacle of power, and he threw off all disguises. He intended to run the country as absolute dictator.

Since fighting continued against him, he occasionally had to take personal charge of his troops. He was indeed a busy man, yet he did not neglect matters concerned with national development. In 1870 he issued a decree that provided free and compulsory education. Previously the government had attempted to provide secondary schools, leaving primary education up to the penniless municipal governments. He declared "that free and obligatory teaching of general and moral principles was to be established, as well as that of reading and writing the mother language, practical arithmetic, the metric system, and of the federal constitution. Free instruction would "further include all the range of human knowledge that the Venezuelan might want to acquire, to be extended gratuitously by the public power in so far as possible."

In 1871 a tax was introduced on revenue stamps on all legal documents to provide income for primary education. The first school built was named after him. Traveling teachers were recruited to visit Venezuela's neglected rural hamlets. This enthusiasm for primary education was, unfortunately, short-lived, and he made no effort to see that it continued growing.

Guzmán Blanco had not taken direct action against the Church until he found that priests were working with his Conservative enemies. He persuaded the archbishop to replace some of the more troublesome priests. After one of his victories in battle with the rebels, a more serious conflict arose. His Minister of the Interior asked the churches to hold *Te Deum* services in celebration of the victory. The archbishop demurred, pointing out that a triumph over one's countrymen was not really something to be celebrated. He suggested that instead Guzmán Blanco should extend complete amnesty to the losers, and then hold a thanksgiving service. Guzmán Blanco was away in the field at the time, or he might have agreed with this suggestion. His Minister of the Interior, however, regarded the archbishop's action as unfriendly, and exiled him. A serious and unnecessary Church-State conflict was thus precipitated.

Knowing that the Church derived its power and influence from its wealth and its control over marriage and over education, Guzmán Blanco proceeded ruthlessly to reduce it to complete dependence upon the state. Compulsory tithes were abolished. The Church had to rely on the government for money. Most Venezuelan presidents have regarded the state's responsibility to the Church as a serious matter, and there have not been many instances of conflict. Although Guzmán Blanco declared that a state-supported Church was incompatible with democracy, it seems likely that if the clergy had supported him enthusiastically he would have felt differently. He simply would not tolerate opposition from any institution or group.

While carrying on his feud with the Church, Guzmán Blanco devoted considerable attention to economic development. Public buildings, including a new residence for the archbishop, were constructed. Roads linked the major cities, and work on the La Guaira–Caracas railroad was pushed. Guzmán Blanco traveled frequently to attend opening ceremonies. Plaques on buildings and bridges gave him credit for the work. Statues of him were erected in many plazas. A multitude of streets were named after him.

In the 1870's Guzmán Blanco was at the peak of his political power and prestige, and his vanity was boundless. In order to ensure his popularity with the masses, he encouraged a cult of Guzmán Blanco. Each year there were essay contests on the subject "La Gloria de Guzmán Blanco," and so many essays were submitted it took three hundred judges to select the winners. The Venezuelan Congress gave him the title of "Illustrious American and Regenerator of Venezuela."

Guzmán Blanco's political machine was powerful, and he frequently let another man serve a term as president while he and his family lived in Paris. Occasionally there was criticism of him

in his absence, and in 1878 mobs demolished his statues in Caracas. His friends rallied to his support, and by early 1879 he was
back in power.

In 1883 there was a tremendous celebration in honor of the
centennial of Bolívar's birth. Delegates attended from all over
Latin America, and some of them could not be sure who was
more honored—Bolívar or Guzmán Blanco. In the same year the
first railroad train arrived in Caracas from the port city of La
Guaira, and another celebration was held. Once more Guzmán
Blanco was the center of attention.

When his term ended, Guzmán Blanco installed General Joaquín Crespo in the presidency and left for Europe as envoy extraordinary. Once more his opponents denounced him. Unrest
became widespread, for poor harvests seriously injured the economy. Guzmán Blanco's friends declared that only he could save
the country, and clamored for his return. In 1886 he was president once more, for the last time. In 1889, while he was in Europe, mobs tore down his statues again. Opposition was so intense
Guzmán Blanco gave up all thought of returning, and lived in
Paris until his death in 1899.

Like most Latin American *caudillos,* Guzmán Blanco was not
all good or all evil. His achievements, compared to those of many
of his predecessors and successors, were substantial. He pacified
the country, promoted education, and pushed economic development, but at his own price. His vanity grew at the same rate as his
power, and he could not brook any opposition or even opinions
different from his own. On one occasion, for example, he decided
to do a favor for the son of one of his friends. He called the young
man to his office, and announced that he was to become an engineer in the Ministry of Public Works. The youth protested that he
was not an engineer.

"How dare you!" Guzmán Blanco replied. "You are an engineer.
You have to be an engineer, and don't argue with me."

"Yes, General, if you order so."

"It is not what I order. It is what I do, and because of this you
are going to take over the office of the director of the Ministry of

Public Works." The appointment was published the next day, and at least one youthful citizen learned the penalty for arguing with the "Illustrious American."

Guzmán Blanco proclaimed himself the spokesman for liberal principles, but this seems to have been more a matter of convenience than of doctrine. His ruthlessness toward the Conservatives appears to have been inspired mainly by the desire for vengeance. He frequently rigged elections and terrorized the opposition, and a number of would-be rivals for the presidency found this ambition to be a fatal malady. Though Guzmán Blanco came into power as leader of the federalists, he practiced autocratic centralism.

It is true that Guzmán Blanco achieved financial reorganization and honest administration in Venezuela, and both were badly needed. His critics maintain that these achievements were not the result of patriotism, but to improve his opportunities for personal gain. A healthy treasury made possible more contracts for public works and better credit abroad, and Guzmán Blanco learned early how to divert part of the contracts and loans to his own account.

Guzmán Blanco's critics also point out that his long regime gave few lasting benefits to the country. Old problems remained unsolved and new ones were added. The Church never recovered its spiritual power. His educational program was abandoned and ignored after the first year or two. Agriculture was not genuinely improved, and the lot of the poorer classes remained as deplorable as ever.

Perhaps if Guzmán Blanco had been succeeded by a regime that continued the programs he initiated, his balance sheet would seem more favorable. But he made no provision for such an administration, and seemed totally unconcerned over Venezuela's future. The result was that the country floundered miserably after his fall, and the presidency became the highest goal of a military career. Half a century passed before Venezuela began to break free from the grip of the military and establish genuine, representative civil government. In the meantime, a succession of military chiefs looted the country on a scale that surpassed the peculations of Guzmán Blanco. For this he is at least partly responsible, to the degree that he established the pattern.

Manuel González Prada
1848–1918

González Prada was born in Lima, the descendant of prominent Spanish and Peruvian families. His mother was a descendant of Antonio de Ulloa, an eighteenth-century Spanish scientist who had been sent on a scientific expedition to South America. His grandfather came to Peru in 1784, and rose to high rank in the royal army. In the struggle for independence, this grandfather supported the royalists.

Francisco Prada, González Prada's father, was born in 1815, and studied law at the University of Chuquisaca in Bolivia. The family lived for a time in Arequipa, then settled in Lima. Francisco Prada was one of the most conservative Peruvians of his generation. He regarded all forms of liberalism with loathing and horror.

Doña Josefa, the mother, was as extremely religious as the father was ultraconservative. Although the Pradas were relatively wealthy, and many distinguished visitors called at their home, the family lived as austerely as monks in a monastery. It was in this somber atmosphere that Peru's great liberal thinker was reared. It is likely that his views were in part a reaction to those of his parents, for he was both liberal to the extreme in politics, and completely opposed to the Church.

For a short time the family lived in Bolivia, but a revolt sent them into exile in Chile. Here González Prada attended the Colegio Inglés, where José Toribio Medina also studied. He learned to read both English and German. After the family returned to Lima, González Prada was enrolled in the Seminary of Santo Toribio. He had no desire to enter the priesthood, and he hated the seminary so violently that he ran away when his parents refused to permit him to withdraw. In 1861 his father reluctantly allowed him to enter the Colegio de San Carlos, which was noted for the open discussions of political and social topics engaged in by its faculty and students. It was here that González Prada began to form his liberal views.

After his father's death González Prada studied law for one year, but only at his mother's urging. For the next eight years he managed the family estate in the Mala Valley. These were years of intensive reading and of experiments and research in chemistry in an effort to discover new uses for local plants. He also wrote and published poetry.

During the War of the Pacific González Prada joined the Army and fought in the defense of Lima against the Chileans. He indicated his growing opposition to the Church by refusing to confess before going into battle. After the war he began attacking the militarists who dominated Peru, and he was also outspoken against the Church and against popular superstitions.

As president of a literary club González Prada made himself well known to Peruvian intellectuals. He won fame as an orator, not because of great speaking ability but for his forceful presentation of bold ideas. He declared that political freedom was not enough, and demanded unlimited freedom in all things. He was, to some degree, an intellectual anarchist.

The literary group he led became the nucleus of a political party, and a forerunner of the Aprista party that was formed after his death. He still felt keenly the humiliating defeat by Chile, and he relentlessly attacked the customs and institutions he felt were responsible for it. The Church was the foremost of these institutions to receive his scathing criticisms, but it was not alone.

Although he was from an aristocratic family, González Prada attacked the aristocracy of Lima as profiteers and plantation owners. The first, he said, should have on its coat of arms a hand reaching into moneybags. The second should have a hand brandishing a whip over the serfs. His attacks on the cherished traditions of a provincial and religious society were disturbing to many. Even some of those who admired his literary talents denounced him for his rebellious and unconventional ideas, and protested that he was creating problems where none had existed.

In 1887 González Prada married a French girl, Adrienne de Verneuil, and she encouraged him to keep up the discouraging battle. At first she shared only his literary views, but she came to share his political liberalism and his religious freethinking as well.

In 1888 González Prada delivered an address that made him the main intellectual leader of Peruvian students. He spoke out against the forces of traditionalism and corruption that kept Peru from developing into a modern, mature nation. In 1891 his followers joined him in organizing the National Union party. Its platform, considered shockingly radical by many at the time, included land for the Indians, a decrease in their taxes, laws to protect workingmen, direct elections, representation of minority parties, and a lessening of the power of the president.

From 1891 to 1898 González Prada and his wife lived in exile in Paris. Here he read deeply in French liberal philosophy, and he became interested in socialism. He traveled to Spain, and became acquainted with the Spanish writers known as the "Generation of '98," who were trying to revive Spain. On his return to Lima he resumed the leadership of his party, but soon left it. By nature he was absolutely uncompromising, and he was irritated at the willingness to compromise on the part of members of his party. He was simply not temperamentally suited to take part in everyday political activity, where many compromises are necessary. By calling for a union of intellectuals and workers, he created at least a part of the framework of the modern Aprista party.

By repeatedly reminding Peruvians of crimes against the Indians, González Prada awakened an intellectual awareness of this basic social problem. "We are," he declared, "accomplishing the miracle of killing in the Indian something that dies hard in man. I mean hope."

González Prada also kept up his attacks on the Church, and protested that liberalism could not exist side by side with Catholicism. He was convinced that the country had more priests and nuns than it could support, and he opposed the coming of foreign priests. "Immigrants who come to exercise a trade or a profession," he wrote in 1903, "have to overcome great obstacles and often are not able to establish themselves. Those who have only a tonsure and a little Latin do not fail to find a spacious nest in which to lodge. . . ."

On another occasion he criticized the shallowness of the Peruvians' religious feelings. "Properly speaking," he said, "we do not have religion, but only religious practices. From the depths of the people to the surface of the ruling class, we find no men animated by a spiritualized belief, but rabbles sunk in the grossest superstitions."

Though there was talk of nominating González Prada for the presidency in 1903, nothing came of it. He was not only unsuited for the role, but it is also unlikely that the Army, the aristocracy, and the Church would have permitted him to govern even if he had been elected. He kept on cheerfully making enemies as well as admirers. One speech called "Women, the Church's Slaves" even alienated his sister Isabel.

If no one had agreed with González Prada he would have been dismissed as a crank, and his writings and speeches would have caused no stir. But many Peruvians shared some of his views if not all of them. Most of them, perhaps, might agree that the Church should be reformed and excluded from politics and control over education, but they did not want to eradicate it completely. He began as a critic of what he considered the corrupt practices of the clergy, and went on to become an atheist and an enemy of religion. He became fanatical in his opposition to the Church, and blamed it for things over which it had no control. He ignored the fact that the Church was a reflection of Peruvian society and that under the circumstances it could hardly be expected to attain perfection unaided. As González Prada's feelings became more intense, however, his criticism became destructive rather than constructive.

"What has Lima become?" he once asked. "A Dead Sea in which the churches and monasteries stand out like islands without water or vegetation. . . . This is a city which includes more than a hundred edifices devoted to worship, and religious education has not a single municipal school worthy of a civilized nation."

It was difficult to find an official position acceptable to him, though the government would have been delighted to send him on diplomatic missions abroad. He was offered various positions, but he refused most of them. Finally, in 1912, he became Director of the National Library. He held this post under a blanket of criticism, and was expelled from it from 1914 to 1916. He returned to it the latter year, and held it till his death in 1918.

Latin Americans have been strong in both praise and condemnation of González Prada. After his death the Peruvian government, in an effort to make his ideas seem less controversial and important, gave them official approval. His speeches and writings were, in fact, keen analyses of a society hampered by its colonial traditions, class distinctions, and exploitation by politicians and Army officers. In passing judgment on Peru, González Prada based his standards on the traditions of ancient Greece and modern France.

Writing in the 1930's, Federico de Onís, the famous Spanish scholar and Columbia University professor, stated that "Manuel González Prada is without doubt one of the first precursors of the present epoch in America, because his spirit, since his youth, was characterized by its nonconformity and its lack of satisfaction." These qualities have appealed to Peruvian students for several generations.

Luis Alberto Sánchez, one of the great Peruvian writers of recent times, wrote his doctoral dissertation at the University of San Marcos on González Prada. In it he sang the praises of his subject. One professor who was on his doctoral committee objected to the choice of subject as unworthy of a serious study. González Prada, he declared, "had been a mediocre poet, a pompous prose writer, a man of questionable conduct, a failure in politics, an ideologist without ideology, and in general an imitator." Others who disagreed with González Prada's ideas and goals held similarly low opinions of his thought and writings.

Many Peruvians, however, have held González Prada in the highest esteem of any of their national heroes, and point out that the painful steps toward progress and change for the better that the country has made were indirectly his work. "He molded the mind of Peruvian youth," said Luis Alberto Sánchez. The Apristas considered him a "purifying flame."

In 1922 "people's universities," to bring higher education within reach of the poor, were founded in Peru. Because of González Prada's urging of a union between intellectuals and laborers, these universities bore his name and perpetuated many of his ideas. Most of his followers abandoned his severe anti-Church, antireligion attitude.

The future leader of the Aprista party, and González Prada's successor as the molder of the minds of Peruvian students, was Víctor Raúl Haya de la Torre. During González Prada's last years Haya de la Torre was a young student leader in the cause of university reform. Though discouraged by the tremendous obstacles and opposition to change, Haya was heartened by his conversations with the old maestro. Because of these conversations, Haya decided that he would also dedicate his life to the cause of reform, social as well as political. Much of Haya's life, as a result, has been spent in prison or in exile, and the Army has intervened more than once to keep him from the presidency.

González Prada was in some ways paradoxical, "a literary man who pinned his hopes on science . . . an aristocrat who learned to look forward to the proletarian revolution . . . the Spaniard of old family who gave the Indian first place among his country's problems . . . the poet who accepted economics." He was the living spirit of national regeneration. He wished his country to be great, and he knew that it could not achieve greatness without first making drastic changes in attitudes, values, and customs. His whole life was a campaign for these changes.

Political corruption and inefficiency infuriated him. He knew from experience that domestic warfare was fruitless. In other lands "revolutions come as a painful but fruitful step in the evolution of the people," he said. In Peru, on the other hand, after Indian soldiers had killed one another, the leaders of both sides got together to divide the spoils.

Lack of popular education was also a drag on Peruvian development. The selfishness and resistance to change on the part of the landowners were others. The pitiful state of commerce and industry, and the vast economic chasm between the classes were still other causes of social stagnation. González Prada made an accurate diagnosis of his country's ills, and he pointed these out repeatedly and in logical terms, so that Peruvians were unable to ignore them indefinitely. He did not cause a revolution, but he started a long, slow struggle for reform that Haya de la Torre and the Aprista party continued. The movement González Prada helped initiate is not likely to end soon.

José Batlle y Ordóñez
1865–1929

Uruguay's history as an independent nation had been marred by constant strife between her two parties, the Colorados (Reds) and the Blancos (Whites). The presidency was a prize won in battle. A "pact of the parties" eventually developed as a crude form of political compromise. This gave the Blancos, who represented the large landowners, control of certain states. The Colorados usually held the presidency. The contest for the presidency was a personal battle, and party doctrines and platforms played little part in the outcome.

Batlle was the son of a former president, and he became interested in politics early. In 1873 he and other students founded a journal, *El Espíritu Nuevo.* Its message was philosophical rather than political, and its purpose was "the total emancipation of the American spirit from the tutelage of the Old World." Batlle was a nationalist even as a youth, and he remained a nationalist throughout his life.

In 1879 he left the University of Montevideo without receiving a degree, and lived in Paris for the next two years. He attended the University of Paris, and he became acquainted with the intellectual currents of western Europe.

On his return to Uruguay, Batlle began writing for various newspapers, and he took part in an unsuccessful revolt against the government. For this action he was imprisoned briefly. He became convinced that peaceful political organization and action were needed. In 1881 he founded a newspaper, *El Día,* and in its columns began a campaign for democracy and truly representative government. The Colorado party, which had supported many dictators, had fallen into decay. Batlle began to revive it and to reorganize it along lines of his own thinking. He made it the party of political, economic, and social reform.

Batlle for a time served as political chief of one of the states, and in the Chamber of Deputies and the Senate. In these offices he demonstrated great administrative ability. He also became the nation's best-known and most influential journalist, and by 1903 his prominence was sufficient to enable him to win the presidency. At this time his main purposes were not well known, and they had nothing to do with his election. He had more prestige than his party, partly because he was the son of a former president, but largely because of his campaign for honest government. Shortly before the election he declared, "I am convinced that the remedy for all our ills lies in electoral freedom, in honest elections."

The Blancos were aroused at his election, and most of his first term was concerned with crushing their rebellion and restoring peace. He was determined to remove the causes for such revolts in the future, and to end the division of the country between the two parties.

In 1907, when his term ended, he went to Europe, and remained there until time for the campaigns of 1911. Once more he won handily, and although the Blancos were apprehensive, they did not revolt.

In 1911 Batlle launched his major reform program, one of the most remarkable of any ever seen in Latin America. In various speeches he made clear his feelings and intentions. As early as 1896 he had stated his attitude toward labor: "We sympathize with the strikers. A strike means that the weak have made themselves strong, and having first implored justice now demand it."

In 1908 he declared: "Every strike is justified and it would be ideal if all could be successful. . . . After all, the workers merely seek a greater share of the wealth they create, and they use no weapon other than that of abstaining from work when they have lost hope of improvement otherwise. If their absence causes great difficulties, it is merely proof of the importance of labor."

At another time he wrote that "modern industry must not be allowed to destroy human beings. The State must regulate it to make more happy the life of the masses." At a time when few governments in Latin America or elsewhere felt that they had any responsibility toward the laboring classes, he advocated direct and positive government action to promote their well-being. He did not seek redistribution of land, though a small percentage of the population owned most of it. He felt that the breakup of the large estates would follow naturally in the wake of his other reforms. He probably was also reluctant to drive the powerful Blancos to rebellion.

Batlle felt that political instability was caused by social problems, maldistribution of wealth, and the concentration of power in the hands of the president. "There is," he said, "great injustice in the enormous gap between the rich and the poor. . . . Our population may be divided into those who have received more than they deserve and those who receive less. . . . But that does not mean that a man is either exploited or an exploiter. The inequality is not deliberate on the part of the more fortunate. . . . Nor is there reason for class hatred, for we all covet riches. . . . The real source of inequality is in the difficulty of arriving at a just distribution. . . . The gap must be narrowed—and it is the duty of the State to attempt that task."

Without political stability, he knew, no reforms could be lasting. He promoted universal suffrage, the secret ballot, and proportional representation as means of making elections more orderly and meaningful. To reduce the power of the president he proposed creation of an executive council to replace the president. In this council would-be presidents could have some part in policy-making without any one man dominating the whole government.

Batlle was unable to push through the type of council-executive he envisioned. Instead a compromise, makeshift arrangement was made, in which the president remained but shared his domestic executive powers with a council. (After Batlle's death, Uruguay abandoned the executive council from 1934 to 1951, but it was restored in the latter year).

Batlle's proposed reforms during his second term included state monopolies in insurance and the production of electrical power, to keep these basic activities out of the hands of foreign companies; the eight-hour day for workmen, university education for women, secondary schools for rural districts, universal free education through the university, and similar matters. Earlier he had pushed through a divorce law and the abolition of the death penalty.

With regard to the nation's economy, Batlle reflected the powerful economic nationalism that was becoming characteristic of Latin America. He was not opposed to investments by foreigners, but he was determined that these investments should not permit outsiders to dominate the economy to the disadvantage of Uruguayans. In 1907 he had written from Paris, "We can make great progress during the next twenty years if we have honest government, and especially if we are less generous in handing out money to foreign corporations."

On his re-election in 1911, in addition to national insurance and electric public utility, he established three state banks and created a port authority. He did not advocate government control of all productive enterprises, but only of those he felt were essential to protect Uruguayans from foreign economic domination.

"From the point of view of the national economy," he once explained, "a wasteful administration by the State is always preferable to the efficient management of an industry by foreign enterprise." The reason for this was that in one case the profits remained in the country. In the other they were taken abroad, for the benefit of others.

Batlle supported the idea of state intervention in the economy, declaring: "The sphere of state intervention is expanding in every civilized country. Modern conditions have increased the number of industries that fall under the heading of public services. . . . Competition has ceased to mean something invariably beneficial, monopoly is not necessarily condemnable. . . . The modern state unhesitatingly accepts its status as an economic organization. It will enter industry when competition is not practicable, when control by private interest vests in them authority inconsistent with the welfare of the state, when a fiscal monopoly may serve as a great source of income to meet urgent tax problems, when the continued export of national wealth is considered undesirable."

Batlle left a deeper imprint on Uruguay than any single individual before or since. There was much opposition to his reforms, and it required tremendous skill and leadership to achieve as much as he did. He remained a vital force in politics even when he was no longer president, with the result that the changes he advocated continued to be made. To reinforce party government and to remove personality from politics, he concentrated on the constitutional changes that created the council-executive.

Uruguay remained a small country with limited economic possibilities. The idealistic picture often given of the little nation greatly exaggerates certain aspects and minimizes the ills. Uruguay is far from a modern utopia, and it is not likely to become one. Uruguay's and Batlle's chief contribution seems to be a demonstration that a turbulent Spanish American nation can become a peaceful one and that Spanish Americans can live in relative peace and mutual satisfaction. This in itself is no small accomplishment.

By 1965 Uruguay had reached an economic crisis, by going too far in providing welfare benefits. One-fourth of those employed worked for the government, and many had retired on pensions at the age of forty-five. Although national production has not increased substantially, government spending has continued to rise drastically. It appears that although the council-type executive has solved the problem of political instability, it has failed completely to provide effective leadership in economic matters, and the country has drifted steadily toward bankruptcy.

PART VIII

The Old and the New in Brazil

Joaquim Nabuco was one of the finest examples of a statesman of the Empire. He came from a plantation family, he was well educated, he was a man of letters and a journalist, and he was a great humanitarian. His greatest achievements were in the struggle to end slavery in Brazil, a struggle to which he devoted nearly twenty years of his life. For Nabuco slavery was a moral issue, and he placed it above political considerations. Because he was a monarchist, Nabuco retired from political life when the republic replaced the monarchy. His prestige and abilities were so great that his country called on him again, to aid in boundary disputes and to serve as Brazil's first ambassador to the United States.

Getúlio Vargas had more to do with transforming Brazil from an agricultural to an industrial nation. The process is not complete, but it is well advanced. Vargas represents the positivist orientation of the state of Rio Grande do Sul extended to the whole nation. When the republic was established, Rio Grande do Sul was the center of the positivist movement. The positivists emphasized science and efficiency in government, and opposed traditional beliefs in democracy and representative government. The positivists in the Army were responsible for creating the republic, but they had not been powerful enough to force a positivist constitution on the nation. The state constitution of Rio Grande do Sul, however, was written according to their desires. All authority was placed in the hands of the governor, with little opportunity for interference from the legislators or the judiciary. Vargas served as governor of Rio Grande do Sul before becoming president.

In order to carry out his program for labor and for economic development, Vargas established a powerful dictatorship. Distasteful as is any dictatorship, it seems unlikely that he could have accomplished much under the government created by the Constitution of 1891. His methods were smooth, and many people in other countries were unaware of the basic harshness of his regime. He preferred mild methods, but he did not shrink from a resort to brutality if it seemed necessary to achieve his purpose.

One of the aspects of the Vargas regime that deserves special emphasis is what occurred after the Army forced him to resign in 1945. He simply returned to Rio Grande do Sul, where he was elected senator. Eventually he won the presidency again. Dictators of Spanish America usually flee for their lives when they are ousted, in order to live abroad on the millions they have stolen and sent to foreign banks. Vargas sought power for patriotic purposes rather than for personal gain. This difference between Vargas and several of his contemporaries in Spanish America is worth noting.

Joaquim Nabuco de Araujo
1849–1910

Joaquim Nabuco, one of Brazil's leading abolitionists and statesmen, came from an old plantation-owning family. His mother's people, the Paes Barretos, first came to the Portuguese colony in 1557, to establish a sugar *fazenda* in Pernambuco. His father's family, the Nabuco de Araujos, came to Bahia in the eighteenth century. After Brazil became an independent empire, the Nabucos were prominent in the legislature. When he was born, on August 19, 1849, his father was a senator.

Nabuco's early years were spent on a sugar *fazenda* at Massangana, owned by his godparents. Even as a child he showed the tendencies that would later lead him to take up the cause of abolition, for he would invariably take the part of any slave who was punished. "It is a work of mercy to punish those who err," his godmother wrote, "but the boy won't let me!"

In 1859 Nabuco went to study under the Baron of Tamphoeus, a Bavarian scholar who had a deep and lasting influence on the youth. The baron wrote to Senator Nabuco, "Joaquim possesses unusual talent; never have I had a pupil of such intelligence." At the age of ten he was sent to the Pedro II School, and he developed such a hatred of boarding schools that he would never send his children to one. He excelled in Latin and Greek, poetry and literature. In 1865 he completed the courses at the Pedro II School and entered the law school at São Paulo.

As a sixteen-year-old law student Nabuco was independent and happy. He immediately took an active interest in politics, and especially in the Liberal party. He wrote for newspapers, and appeared at trials to speak for the defense. Among his friends were Ruy Barbosa, who became a world-famous jurist and principal author of the 1891 Constitution, and Castro Alves, one of Brazil's great poets. All three became ardent abolitionists. This same class at São Paulo law school contained two future presidents, Rodrigues Alves and Afonso Penna.

In 1869 Nabuco went to Recife for his fourth year of law. He was not pleased with his professors, calling them "pools of stagnant water from the Middle Ages. . . ." During this period he became obsessed with the evils of slavery, which he blamed for Brazil's backwardness. He wrote his father: "I want your name to be found under the decree that does away with slavery. . . . I dream of no other glory for you than that of Abraham Lincoln!"

Recife was a center of the plantation aristocracy to which Nabuco belonged. Few shared his views on slavery, yet he did not hesitate to express them. On one occasion he defended a slave against a charge of murder. For slaves the death penalty was usual, and there was no hope of clemency. Nabuco's moving defense, however, won the slave a lighter sentence.

Too young at twenty-one to enter politics, Nabuco served briefly in his father's law office in Rio de Janeiro. One of his first cases was a client who deceived him. On learning of the deceit, Nabuco denounced his client publicly and retired from practicing law. For a time he tried his hand at journalism. Though he believed a constitutional monarchy was the ideal form of government, he did not hesitate to criticize the emperor. He urged Dom Pedro to visit the United States, to learn at first hand the privileges of American citizens, and to see that a country could not be great with slavery. He wrote in favor of separation of Church and State, preferring a "national religion" to an official church.

Nabuco spent the year 1873–1874 in Europe, visiting museums, castles, and churches. He also gained introductions to statesmen and writers, and made several lasting friendships. By 1875 he was ready to abandon his literary pleasures for a more serious career. The Conservative party was in power at the time, and under the electoral system of imperial Brazil a Liberal had little chance of winning. In April, 1876, he was named attaché to the Brazilian legation in Washington. He found New York especially fascinating, and had ample time for following American political contests. In October, 1877, he was transferred to the Brazilian legation in London.

In 1878 the Liberal party came to power, but the year was saddened by the death of Nabuco's father. In the elections Nabuco won a seat in the Chamber of Deputies. Loving travel, he was reluctant to give up his diplomatic career, but he soon embraced the challenge of political life. This was his true calling. In his first campaign speech he marked out the course of his future action. "The great question for Brazilian democracy is not the monarchy; it is slavery," he declared. The audience hissed and booed, but Nabuco was confident.

Weakened by a forty-day attack of typhoid fever, Nabuco

made his first speech before the Chamber. In discussing the rights of non-Catholics in Brazil, he said that "the right of the minority, the right of a single man in relation to his religion, is as perfect as the right of all."

Ideas were always more important to him than men. "Ministers last only a day," he said, "and principles survive." He protested that the Liberal party had no liberal ideas. He wished his party to embrace the goals of direct elections, religious freedom, and emancipation. Freedom was his highest ideal, freedom not only for slaves but for all men. In one of his speeches, he declared that "what makes a people free is simply the fervent desire for freedom, it is the instinct, the feeling that causes it to put forth every effort and to make every sacrifice in order to . . . win it."

In 1871, before Nabuco entered the Chamber, the Rio Branco Law of Free Birth had been passed. Thereafter the children of slaves were to become free after a period of service to their masters. The law was at first welcomed and generally approved, but Nabuco and other abolitionists grew dissatisfied. Nabuco's father had helped push the law through. Two years later, Nabuco asked that something be done about those slaves not affected by the law. Having "redeemed the future generations," Nabuco said, "it was necessary to satisfy the impatience of the present generation." Senator Saraiva agreed: "The great injustice of the law is its failure to care for the present generation."

It was not until 1879 that the slavery question began to be debated seriously in the Congress. Thereafter Nabuco customarily referred to the issue in all his speeches, even though the debate concerned other matters.

In 1880 the abolitionists began to pool their efforts and to accelerate the tempo of their propaganda. Among them were José do Patrocinio and André Rebouças. The latter was a descendant of slaves, and a famous engineer. He became one of the leaders among the abolitionists. Ever an idealist, he served as treasurer of the Anti-Slavery Society and the Abolitionist Confederation, which meant that he paid most of the bills out of his own pocket.

Although he had republican leanings, he became a staunch mon-archist out of gratitude for final emancipation, and even followed the emperor into exile.

Nabuco was not re-elected in 1881, for he refused to campaign seriously. "The practice of begging for votes is absurd, pernicious, and completely out of harmony with the true principles of repre-sentative government," he wrote. "It is as much in the interest of the constituents to choose well as it may be in the interest of the candidate to be chosen." For the first time since independence there was no Nabuco de Araujo in the Congress.

As London correspondent for the *Jornal do Comércio*, Na-buco lived the next two years in London, his favorite of all cities. His spare time was spent in the British Museum learning every-thing he could about slavery everywhere it had existed. Fully armed with facts and figures, he wrote *The Emancipation Move-ment* (*O Abolicionismo*). He began by giving a history of slavery, its legal, social, and human aspects, and its influence on Brazil. He pointed out that the slaveowners had tried to identify Brazil with slavery, so that anyone who attacked it was regarded as an enemy of his country. The book had a tremendous impact in Bra-zil, but, like *Uncle Tom's Cabin*, it was written to serve one pur-pose. After that purpose was served, it was no longer of general interest.

In 1884 Nabuco returned from his self-imposed exile, for his friends protested his absence and demanded his presence in the Chamber of Deputies. The Liberals at last had accepted emanci-pation as a part of their party platform. The propaganda cam-paign was intensified, with a series of lively newspaper articles signed by "Garrison" (Nabuco), "Grey" (Barbosa), "Clarkson" (Gusmão Lobo), taking the names of prominent American and British abolitionists.

When Nabuco arrived in Rio de Janeiro from Recife to take his seat in the Chamber, there was a tremendous reception awaiting him. A number of elections had been disputed, and Nabuco was barred by three votes. The Chamber was almost evenly divided, and a tie vote resulted on a measure to free slaves of sixty years or more of age. The slaveowners wished to be paid for the loss, but refused to ask for compensation.

An election was pending in Pernambuco. Both candidates withdrew in favor of Nabuco. He won easily. Said an editorial in *O Pais:* "Never has any other deputy entered parliament with greater moral strength or surrounded with greater prestige." Nabuco had not even had time enough to visit Pernambuco before the election.

The question of freeing slaves over sixty was revived, and a compromise raised the age to sixty-five. The abolitionists were furious with the law, and called it "the monster." Joaquim Serra called it a pact "between the timid and the obstinate . . . ," a "happy medium between the minimum and nothing." After the law was passed, the Liberal ministry resigned. Dom Pedro named a Conservative, the Baron of Cotegipe, as prime minister. Cotegipe called for new elections, to replace the Liberal majority with one of his own party.

The Conservatives were determined to defeat Nabuco and other abolitionists by any means possible, and only nineteen Liberal deputies were allowed to take their places in the Chamber. The others had been beaten by fraud or had been disbarred on some technicality. The proslavery forces were in complete control, and the abolitionists were eclipsed. Nabuco turned once more to journalism to make his views known. He became editor of *O Pais.*

In 1886 he wrote a series of pamphlets. Most widely read was one called "The Error of the Emperor." The error, Nabuco pointed out, was in changing ministries from Liberal to Conservative. "On the previous day," he wrote, "emancipation was in power, while on the following day slavery was triumphant. This was . . . the fatal error of the Emperor. It was the error of changing his mind, of making the work that was begun useless, and of paralyzing the national movement."

While editor of *O Pais,* Nabuco carried on a number of campaigns. He attacked the practice of whipping as punishment for criminal slaves, while the Minister of Justice defended it. Nabuco called it "a justification of the penalty of death by whipping . . . a disguised death penalty, secure from imperial clemency and cruel in the last degree." He publicized the case of four slaves of Paraíba do Sul who were condemned to receive three hundred lashes each. Two of the four died as a result of the whipping. Nabuco's publicity caused the Senate to abolish whipping. "It will be sad for the Imperial Princess," he wrote, "to read this news on her birthday, and I am profoundly sorry to have to publish it today. However, that picture will enable the future Empress to recognize the condition of our slaves and to understand the mission of the abolitionists in her father's kingdom."

In the election of 1887 the police prevented Nabuco from speaking. Alarmed at abolitionist sentiment, Baron Cotegipe ordered a warship to Recife, but it was wrecked en route. Nabuco won despite all efforts to prevent his supporters from voting.

Another of his campaigns was to relieve the Army of the disagreeable task of pursuing fugitive slaves. The Army, which had reluctantly but dutifully complied with its orders, supported him. Nabuco called anyone who helped recapture fugitive slaves "slave hounds." The Military Club petitioned Dona Isabel, who was serving as regent while Dom Pedro was in Europe, to allow the Army to confine itself to its proper mission. She agreed.

Some patriotic slaveowners, such as Antônio Prado, were moved to free their own slaves and to urge others to do so. Prado also suggested a high tax on slaves, to make their labor unprofitable, but this measure did not pass.

Toward the end of 1887 Nabuco was in Europe again. He planned to return by way of the American South and the Caribbean islands, to study the effects of emancipation in those regions. He wanted proof that emancipation would not, as his enemies claimed, destroy agriculture completely. He was still preoccupied with emancipation, but now he was certain success was near.

While in Europe Nabuco conceived a plan to hasten the emancipation law. Dona Isabel was still serving as regent, and she was known to be extremely devout. Nabuco hastened to Rome, and gained an audience with Pope Leo XIII.

"I was going to the United States," Nabuco said, "where the greatest part of the Negro race in America is located. But then our bishops began to speak with determination and in common accord about the jubilee of Your Holiness and to ask for the emancipation of the slaves as the best and highest means of solemnizing that event in Brazil. When I heard this, I thought that above all else I must come to Rome to ask Your Holiness to complete the work of those prelates by issuing a condemnation of slavery by the Church. This action . . . would give the abolitionists a point of support in the Catholic conscience of the country that would be of the greatest advantage. . . ."

The Pope agreed wholeheartedly and promised to issue an encyclical. Nabuco urged that he do so before May, when the Brazilian Congress would open. The Cotegipe ministry, through the Brazilian legation in Rome, tried in vain to prevent the action. In Brazil, when the Pope's intentions were known, there were wholesale emancipations by individuals and by cities and states.

Cotegipe resigned, and Dona Isabel replaced him with another Conservative, João Alfredo Corrêa de Oliveira, although the Liberals were the party of abolition and should have been given the ministry. The Conservatives resented what they knew they must do, and the Liberals were angry at being deprived of the victory they had won. Some spoke of opposing the Conservative cabinet.

Nabuco disagreed, and declared that he intended to cross party lines and support the ministry. "Our obligation is to free the slaves. They are neither Liberals nor Conservatives and they do not question who their saviors are."

On May 8th the government's proposal was presented to the Chamber. It was simple and direct, and made no mention of compensation for loss of slaves. The law said: "Slavery in Brazil is declared extinct. All dispositions to the contrary are revoked."

The law was passed by both houses and signed on May 13th. This was Sunday, but Brazilians could not wait another day. Eight days of wild celebrations followed.

All other major reforms had been delayed for years because of the abolitionist movement. As soon as this problem was settled, federalism, republicanism, and separation of Church and State became live issues. Nabuco devoted his attention to federalism, for he was certain the Empire would not long survive otherwise. "The truth is," he said, "that today there is only one reform that can hold back the coming of the republic, and that is the autonomy of the provinces."

The Republicans also desired federalism, and the two ideas were closely associated. Few men could accept the idea of a federalized monarchy. Nabuco's enthusiasm for the Empire did not waver, but the former slaveowners were still resentful, and turned their backs. The Empire had failed them in their hour of need. Let it fall! Perhaps compensation for their losses might have won back their support, but it was not forthcoming.

Republican sentiment grew rapidly, and Nabuco withdrew from action to assume the role of spectator. In April, 1889, he married Dona Evelina Torres Ribeiro, and together they visited Argentina and Paraguay. Even though he did not wish to run for his seat in the Chamber, he was elected easily. On November 15th the Army overthrew the Empire and declared Brazil a republic. There was no resistance, for most Brazilians were not aware of what was happening.

Nabuco, feeling that his political career had ended, and doubtful about the Republic's future, went once more to London. He remained there until 1891, when Rodolfo Dantas founded a monarchist newspaper, O Jornal do Brasil, in Rio, and asked Nabuco to join his staff. On the paper were other of his comrades of the abolitionist movement. They disguised their monarchist views discreetly and aimed at quality writing. The paper became widely popular, and the doctrinaire Republicans developed a fierce hatred for it. The government announced that it could not protect the paper against threatened destruction. Dantas and Nabuco left the paper and sailed for Europe. On his return, Nabuco entered law practice.

After the naval revolt of 1893–1894 failed, the hopes of the monarchists were ended. Thereafter Nabuco tried to reconcile his views with those of the new Republic, though he still preferred a constitutional monarchy. For ten years he devoted his time to writing. In 1897 he accepted the post of minister to London, and represented Brazil in the boundary dispute with Great Britain over British Guiana. Victor Emmanuel III of Italy was chosen to arbitrate the dispute. Although Nabuco presented fifteen volumes of documents and a two-thousand-page statement, the decision was more favorable to England than to Brazil.

Nabuco regarded the arbitral award as a personal defeat, but no Brazilian criticized him. As Oliveira Lima wrote to him: "There was greater sadness over the disappointment it meant to you than over the loss of the territory." Ruy Barbosa, the famous jurist, declared: "The defense of our claims made by Joaquim Nabuco is a marvelous work of colossal patience, criticism, argumentation, and genius. This one work would have been enough to earn him fame and honor."

The arbitral decision was made in 1904. A few days later Nabuco wrote to his wife from Rome that an earthquake had occurred. "It was," he wrote, "a telegram from Rio Branco [Brazilian Foreign Minister] offering me Washington."

The United States government had recently agreed to Mexico's raising her legation in Washington to the rank of embassy, and had elevated the American diplomatic mission in Mexico to similar status. Rio Branco assumed that the United States would extend the same courtesy to Brazil, and wanted an especially distinguished man in the post. Nabuco agreed with him that Brazil's foreign policy should be based on a close and friendly relationship with the United States. "The Monroe Doctrine lays down a definite foreign policy for the United States which is now beginning to take shape, and it lays down a similar policy for us. Under such conditions our diplomacy should receive its principal impetus from Washington. Such a policy would be better than the largest army or navy. . . .

"For me the Monroe Doctrine . . . signifies that politically we have broken away from Europe. . . . In that sense I am a Monroist."

In Washington, Nabuco became a popular figure, and his oratorical gifts made him much in demand as a speaker. Most of his efforts the first year were devoted to making preparations for the Third Pan American Conference, to be held in Rio de Janeiro in 1906. In order to enhance the importance of the meeting, Elihu Root decided to attend it in person. This was the first time an American Secretary of State went abroad on an official visit. President Theodore Roosevelt assured Nabuco that Root's decision to attend the conference was caused by the favorable impression Nabuco had made.

In 1906 Nabuco made a nine-thousand-mile trip around the United States and Canada in a private railroad car offered him by Richard Cutts Shannon. He wrote numerous letters to his wife describing his delights at the Grand Canyon, the Cave of the Winds, and other spots of scenic beauty. He saw the remains of San Francisco after the earthquake. "Ruins," he wrote, "do not fit into the American scene; whoever desires to see ruins in the United States should hurry along."

The Rio Conference was a great success. Nabuco was elected president of the conference, and presided over the main sessions. The delegates voted to establish a permanent secretariat in Washington, and Andrew Carnegie gave money to build the Pan American Union building.

Nabuco continued at his Washington post, though his health grew progressively worse. He helped settle two serious disputes, one between the United States and Brazil over a proposed tariff on coffee, the other between the United States and Chile. He kept on with his official duties, though his ill-health forced him to curtail his social activities. On January 17, 1910, he died in Washington.

Nabuco's death was mourned, not only in Washington, where he had made so many friends, but universally. After impressive ceremonies, his body was taken to Brazil on board an American battleship, the U.S.S. *North Carolina*. A few days before his death he had written to his sister: "The only way in which I do not want to cross the ocean is in a coffin." He had hoped to return home before his death, but it came too suddenly. He made, in fact, two voyages—to Rio de Janeiro, and to his final resting place, his native Recife.

Getúlio Dornelles Vargas

1883–1954

The Brazilian border state of Rio Grande do Sul, where Getúlio Vargas was born, is a region much influenced by neighboring Uruguay and Argentina. The Riograndenses were cattlemen and fighters. Vargas's father had been a colonel in the Paraguayan War, and in 1898 Vargas himself joined the Army as a private. His unit was sent to the Bolivian border for a time, during the dispute over Acre Territory. When his enlistment ended, Vargas entered the law college in Pôrto Alegre.

After earning his law degree, Vargas served as deputy in the state legislature. He became much involved in political activity. Rio Grande do Sul was the region of Brazil where the Positivism of Auguste Comte attracted the strongest following during the Empire. When the Republic was established, Rio Grande do Sul drew up a state constitution along Positivist lines. This meant that the state president exercised considerable authority and that representative government was sacrificed in the name of efficiency. It was in this political situation that Vargas received his training and experience in government.

As a prominent Riograndense, Vargas served on the National Commission of Finances. President Washington Luis, who assumed office in 1926, named him Minister of Finance. After a year in this office Vargas resigned to become president of the state of Rio Grande do Sul. He promised reforms, toleration, and peace; and he attracted enthusiastic support. He had been chosen because of a political conflict, and he showed great skill in bringing the opposing sides together.

In 1929 a presidential campaign was begun to choose a successor for Washington Luis. Because São Paulo and Minas Gerais were the largest and wealthiest states, it had become customary to alternate the presidency between Paulistas and Mineiros. Washington Luis was a Paulista, and it was the turn of the Mineiros.

The world-wide depression began this same year, and Washington Luis felt that only another Paulista could carry out his economic policies. He broke the unwritten agreement with the Mineiros, and he threw his support behind Júlio Prestes of São Paulo. The Mineiros were enraged. Joining groups in other states, they formed the Liberal Alliance. The candidate of this new party was Getúlio Vargas. When the election had been held, the government announced that Prestes had won. The Liberal Alliance charged that the government had used fraud and intimidation.

In October, 1930, before the new term began, revolts broke out in Rio Grande do Sul and Minas Gerais. Vargas led his own state's forces in the march northward. Revolts soon broke out in other states. On October 23rd the Army stepped in and asked Washington Luis to resign. A few days later, he was on his way to Europe, and the rebels had triumphed.

The Army had perhaps planned to remain in power, but popular demonstrations in behalf of Vargas were so enthusiastic it turned over the government to him as provisional president.

Brazil was facing a severe economic crisis, and the problems were many. Vargas first had to restore order and to give his rule some basis for legality. The Paulistas, furthermore, were angry at seeing their candidate lose the presidency. In 1932 São Paulo rebelled, demanding a return to constitutional rule. The revolt was put down, but it was costly.

One reason for animosity toward the government was that Vargas had replaced most governors with "interventors" who were loyal to him. In order to placate the growing opposition, Vargas agreed to call an assembly to draft a constitution. The assembly completed its work in 1933, and it elected Vargas as constitutional president.

The Constitution of 1934 was a step toward creation of a corporate state—a government in which groups and professions would be represented rather than political parties. Some of the members of the Chamber of Deputies were to be elected by professional groups. Vargas was never satisfied with this constitution, but its adoption gave him a few years in which to prepare one for his "New State."

The world depression still ran its course, and everywhere extremist groups of right and left arose. Communist agitators advocated their solutions to economic and political problems. At the opposite end of the political spectrum, the extremists of the right organized to combat communists. In some countries, such as Fascist Italy and Nazi Germany, the extremists of the right seized power. They made a similar attempt in Brazil, but failed.

The Integralista party of Brazil was similar to its prototypes in Italy and Germany. Its members wore green shirts, clicked heels, and paraded. They drilled like a regular army and collected weapons for use when the time came to capture the government. They hated communism, democracy, Masonry, liberalism, Americans, and Jews. Vargas watched their parades impassively, without smile or frown. One of his greatest political assets was his keen sense of timing and his ability to wait for the proper moment. His reserved attitude toward the Integralistas deluded them into thinking he favored them and would allow them one day to take over Brazil. Perhaps he smiled inwardly at their foolishness.

The Constitution of 1934 did not permit the president to be reelected immediately. In 1937 the presidential elections were approaching. One by one Vargas induced the would-be candidates to withdraw, all but Plínio Salgado, leader of the green shirts. The Integralistas rejoiced, feeling victory must surely be theirs.

On November 11, 1937, Vargas astonished the country by abolishing all political parties, canceling the election, and replacing the Constitution of 1934 by a new one. The Constitution of 1937 ushered in the New State, and it contained the goals of the Vargas régime.

The New State was vastly different from previous governments of Brazil. Already, in 1935, São Paulo had begun industrial development. Modernizing Brazil's economy and society were two major aims of the régime. It sought economic nationalism, executive centralism, and an integrated society.

Vargas was no imitator of other men or their systems. He was a practical politician, not bound to any particular system. He intended to rule Brazil to achieve the New State's goals, and toward this end he was willing to adopt or invent techniques, some of which were copied by others.

Immediately after proclaiming the New State, Vargas sent military interventors to replace the state governors, and the states were reduced to provinces. The purpose was to achieve centralization of control.

It cannot be said that Vargas ruled according to the Constitution of 1937, for it was never actually promulgated. He did, however, rule according to the principles it contained. To understand it, however, it should be read from the end to the beginning, making the last article first.

Article 187 states: "This Constitution comes into effect on the day it is dated and will be submitted to a national plebiscite in the form regulated in a decree of the President of the Republic."

Article 186: "A state of emergency is declared for the whole country."

Article 180: "Until the National Parliament convenes, the President of the Republic shall be empowered to issue decree laws on all legislative matters of the Union."

Article 178: "As of this date, the Chamber of Deputies, the Federal Senate, the Legislative Assemblies of the States, and the Municipal Chambers are dissolved. The elections for the National Parliament will be set by the President of the Republic, after the plebiscite referred to in Art. 187 has taken place."

With a state of emergency declared in the Constitution, no

plebiscite could be held or a congress elected. The President was authorized to rule by decree during a state of emergency, and this is what Vargas did until his fall in 1945. In that year a Brazilian cartoon showed a child asking its father what an election is. "I don't know," the father replied. "Ask Grandfather."

During the Vargas era one rarely read unfavorable comments on him in Brazil or abroad. He developed a unique and effective system of censorship. The government made newsprint a monopoly. Newspaper editors were warned what not to print. If they ignored the warning, they soon found themselves without newsprint. This system proved simpler and less troublesome than having everything censored before it was printed.

Foreign correspondents were treated quite differently. On arrival they were greeted like visiting dignitaries, and were showered with honors and favors and entertainment as long as their reports on Brazil were friendly and uncritical. This method, too, was successful. If any foreign journal criticized the régime it was simply banned; and foreign correspondents who were critical were packed off for home.

In Brazil, opponents of the régime were treated harshly. Vargas was determined to carry out his program, and those who opposed him did so at their own risk. But despite the underlying harshness of the police state, it was managed so smoothly that many people were unaware of the harsh aspect.

Brazil industrialized with astonishing speed under Vargas. By 1938 industrial production was double the value of agricultural production. This process was greatly accelerated in Brazil by the needs of the Allies during World War II.

The outbreak of the war posed serious problems for Vargas. He had demonstrated his scorn for political democracy and representative government, under which Brazil had floundered ineptly from 1890 to 1930. He had broken up the Integralistas, who had been working with the Ambassador of Nazi Germany against him, and who tried to assassinate him in 1938. He needed to know who was most likely to win. During this first half of 1942, Brazilian newspapers were allowed to play up German victories over Russia, British victories over Germany, and any victories of the United States over any foe. The result was that Brazilian readers were given a distorted view of the conflict.

On one occasion Vargas made a speech in which he compared "vigorous new states" to "decadent liberals." Oswaldo Aranha and other Brazilian diplomats had a difficult time trying to explain that the "decadent liberals" were not Great Britain, France, and the United States. Yet once Vargas decided to join the Allies, he did so with his usual thoroughness. He reminded the Allies that while they had done nothing to check the rise and spread of fascism, in 1938 he had crushed the Integralistas.

As the war continued, Brazilians grew more and more restless, for they were fighting on the side of liberty and democracy, yet they were denied these at home. In one protest against censorship, students of the São Paulo Law School paraded with their mouths fastened closed with adhesive tape. Police opened fire on them; no one knows how many were killed, for the newspapers were silenced on the subject. Protest of any sort was not allowed.

In 1945, partly because of pressure from the United States, Vargas promised to hold elections. Before the elections were held, the Army became worried that he might be planning another coup to remain in power. The Army called on him to resign, and he complied. He simply returned to São Paulo, where he was elected senator. Most Latin American dictators who leave office alive flee for their lives. They then enjoy life abroad on their Swiss bank accounts or investments in Miami real estate.

It is no simple matter to reach an objective conclusion as to the merits and demerits of the Vargas régime, for there are too many aspects to be considered. Probably most Brazilians would argue that the changes could have been accomplished under a democratic and representative political régime, but there is little in Brazil's history before Vargas to support this view. On the other hand, for those who cherish liberty, democracy, and representative government above economic affairs—and many Brazilians do—the régime was unbearable. Whatever else may be said, dictatorships for whatever purpose have little to recommend them.

Some have compared Vargas to Perón, to the great advantage of Vargas. He did not become a multimillionaire through graft, nor was his sincerity ever doubted. Both employed the same methods, and Perón even copied the Brazilian method of censorship. On one occasion, Perón said, "When we are called fascists in the American press, we look at our northern neighbor, and smile." The Vargas régime was always given favorable treatment by American newspapers. The Perón regime was under constant attack. Brazil co-operated with the Allies. Argentina—the government but not the people—favored the Axis. The Vargas dictatorship was suave and smooth. That of Perón had a crude, stormtrooper, rubber-truncheon character.

Probably we are too close to the events to be completely objective. The process of industrialization in every society has caused much human suffering. We have forgotten the suffering that occurred in our country and others when they underwent the same process of change from agriculture to industry, but the suffering was massive. The passage of time seems to dull these human pains. If Brazil achieves her industrial potential, the consensus probably will be that Vargas' methods were unquestionably justified.

It would have been better for his reputation as a skillful politician if he had resisted the temptation to seek the presidency in 1950. That he won after only one intervening term is a tribute to the rise of labor and the shortness of human memories. He ran as the candidate of the Brazilian Labor party.

Governing with a Congress in which selfish and partisan interests prevailed over those of the nation was quite different from ruling by decree.

Inflation was the major economic problem. It raged unchecked. Vargas declared his intention of serving as an "elder statesman," above the political strife; but an active, effective political leader was needed far more than a philosopher. Brazil drifted, and conditions worsened. A rising note of protest was heard, and there were demands that Vargas take a leave of absence.

In 1954 this unrest and irritation turned into a national crisis over an incident and its aftermath. Carlos Lacerda, the most outspoken critic of the government, was shot at by an assassin in front of his home on Tonoleros Street in Rio de Janeiro. There had been other attempts on his life, and young Air Force officers who were off duty took turns accompanying him for his protection. On this occasion Major Ruben F. Vaz drove off the assassin, but was killed.

The driver of the getaway car was soon captured, and he named a member of the presidential guard as the man who had hired him. A manhunt began that included airplanes, cars, and bloodhounds. The man was captured, and he told all. Involved were other members of the palace guard, men who had served Vargas even before 1930. Scandal followed scandal. The chief of the palace guard, who had been with Vargas for thirty years, had accumulated a tremendous fortune on a surprisingly modest salary. In one pocket of a suit hanging in his closet was cash equal to about $4,000. It was apparently a trifling sum, for he had "forgotten about it." As the testimony continued, it was learned that he had accumulated his vast wealth through pay-offs for his influence and a dozen other illegal activities. The police report on the case was a huge catalogue of crime and corruption. On reading the report, Vargas, whose honesty has never been questioned, said, "I have the impression that I am over a sea of mud." His quarters in the National Palace were directly over those of the guard. He was obviously shaken at the betrayal by men he had trusted.

The scandals raised popular discontent to a dangerous level. An attempt to impeach Vargas failed, for he had not broken any law. The Air Force high command began demanding that Vargas resign. The Army chiefs were divided. On August 18th Vice President Café Filho suggested that both he and Vargas resign. Vargas replied that the only way he would leave Catete Palace was feet first.

On August 22nd the Air Force officers, joined by some Army officers, issued the "Brigadiers' Manifesto," a demand that Vargas resign for the sake of the country. By August 23rd the Army and Navy had both joined the Air Force. At 2:00 A.M. on the 24th, the cabinet met at Catete Palace to discuss the crisis with Vargas.

No one had any helpful suggestion. The military ministers admitted that only a small part of the armed forces was still loyal. Civilian ministers suggested a leave of absence or resignation or submission of the matter to an assembly of state governors. They could not reach any agreement. Said Vargas: "Since you have not arrived at a decision, I will accept the leave of absence. But if you come to depose me, you will find my body."

The high command of the armed forces was also meeting to learn of the outcome. The cabinet meeting ended at 5:00 A.M., and the officers were told of the plan to take a leave of absence. They refused to accept this, for the state of the nation was too critical. Vargas must resign.

At 8:15 A.M. Getúlio's brother Benjamim awakened him and told him of the generals' decision. "Then it means I have been deposed."

"I don't know if you're deposed," Benjamim replied, "but it's the end."

Vargas then sent him away on an errand.

At 8:30 his valet heard a shot and rushed into the room. Vargas lay on the bed. Near him was a note that said: "To the wrath of my enemies I leave the legacy of my death. I carry with me the sorrow of not having been able to do for the humble all that I desired."

INDEX

219